How To Become An
Ambassador

An American Foreign Service Odyssey

U.S. Ambassador
Thomas Hart Armbruster

For Kathy, Bryan, and Kalia, my fellow travelers who are always with me.

© Thomas Armbruster 2020

ISBN: 978-1-09830-848-3

eBook ISBN: 978-1-09830-849-0

The views expressed are the author's and do not necessarily reflect
the views of the U.S. Department of State.

CONTENTS

INTRODUCTION

The old pilot looked over at me from the right seat apologetically. "I can't not fly." Climbing into the two-seater at his age was obviously not easy. He settled into his seat, I taxied down the Stinson Airport runway, breathing in the 100-degree Texas heat and prop plane fumes, and we were off. In the first year after leaving the Foreign Service I was still trying to figure out what to do. Flying was a good interim step. But, just as for the old pilot, I can't not travel. I've gone back to the State Department now leading inspection teams to Nepal, Bangladesh, Mauritania, Chad, Colombia, and Denmark. This book is for those of you who are curious about the world, and sure that there is a place for you in the international firmament. Why not ambassador? I hope this proves to be a little bit of a flight plan for you on how to get there. In today's uncertain world, I know one thing, we need you. Every one of you; everyone and anyone, from as diverse backgrounds as possible, first and second-generation Americans included. I know there are dreamers out there who would be good ambassadors.

As much as a "How-to" book I hope this is also a "Why-to" book. For me it was adventure, service, environmental cooperation... You'll join with your own ideals and expectations. Don't lose them. One ambassador I visited was being criticized for saying yes to every invitation. As a friend I wrote to him about his staff's concerns, among them, long trips on weekends with a lot of security and that the ambassador did things for "reasons known only to the ambassador." I asked him about it because I had a feeling there was more to it than what meets the eye. He was a former Marine and I knew he did some things out of a sense of commitment and simply because someone had asked, and he had said yes, thus sticking by his word. He got the message on taxing his staff, but there was something important in his thinking that none of us had connected. He said,

On events I attend for reasons known only to me, they almost always involve children or young people. I'm at one now handing out awards at a primary school. By myself, with no public diplomacy staff or control officer. More than any policy advanced, VIP visit, or other issue, our lasting legacy is how we treated and encouraged, if not inspired, young people."

While the steps in this book are not literal checklist items for you, they do add up to just about exactly the amount of effort, sacrifice, commitment, and luck you need to make it. I hope you'll feel inspired.

Buckle up, grab the joystick, let's go!

PART I –
Political Appointee

There are two ways to become an American ambassador. One, is to be a political appointee. The steps follow:

STEP 1 – RAISE A LOT OF MONEY FOR THE SUCCESSFUL PRESIDENTIAL

CANDIDATE

STEP 2 – BECOME WELL AND FAVORABLY KNOWN TO THE CANDIDATE

STEP 3 – DON'T SAY OR DO ANYTHING TO RUIN YOUR SENATE CONFIRMATION

There is a second way to do it which is more circuitous, fun, and demanding. Step 1 for me was getting on a plane at age 17 to Moscow.

Moscow, Russia.

August 31, 1975

My Moscow Journal

Flying over Russia was strangely enough rather like flying over the Midwest. It was very flat between Copenhagen and Moscow and almost totally farmland. Dirt roads outlined the area. The pilot told us when we were over Soviet soil and advised us not to take pictures from the plane or of the airport.

During the flight over I didn't sleep because a man in front of me kept whistling. I tried to watch "The Four Musketeers" but I was too busy to enjoy it. Overall the flight was nice.

I doubt Russia has changed much culturally since 1945, at least not in fashions. The apartment is nice on the inside but looks like one of St. Louis's projects on the outside. I miss my family and wish we hadn't had such a bad connection over the phone today. The market is fascinating and only a few blocks away. The produce isn't great, but the atmosphere is. We have a great three-sided view of Moscow. The soldiers, Russian, are about my age, and our guard seems like a nice guy. He directed me to the apartment after I got lost.

PART II –
Career Foreign Service Officer

STEP 1 – GET A PASSPORT, GO TO MOSCOW

You'll get a black passport with gold letters when you join the State Department. Until then, get your nice blue American passport and go somewhere. Anywhere. There is no requirement that you travel overseas, or speak a language, or have a certain degree, but the testers want to know that you will be successful overseas in a stressful, fast-paced, foreign environment. So, test yourself. My first experience overseas blew my mind.

There are no shortcuts, other than to be a political ambassador. Even if you have a 20-military career behind you, you still start at the visa window. You're a lawyer? Great, visa window. PhD? You get it, you adjudicate visas. Consular work is a good introduction to what we do, how to say no, the importance of languages, and helping out Americans. Looking out for American citizens is everyone's job but especially Consular officers who visit Americans in prison, help out with adoptions, and send the remains of Americans home when they die abroad. You will do a Consular tour on your first or second Foreign Service tour.

This interview by Mark Tauber of the Association for Diplomatic Studies and Training, interspersed throughout, is part of a "frontlines of diplomacy" project archived in the Library of Congress. My story is about a typical Foreign Service field guy with a special interest in the environment. There are many other stories. War stories. High diplomacy. Intrigue… If you are a foreign policy junkie, there is plenty of dope in the Library of Congress.

INTERVIEW

The Association for Diplomatic Studies and Training Foreign
Affairs Oral History Project

AMBASSADOR THOMAS HART ARMBRUSTER

Interviewed by: Mark Tauber
Initial Interview Date: November 28, 2018
Copyright 2019 ADST

Q: Today is Wednesday, November 28, 2018. We are having our first session with Ambassador Thomas Armbruster. Ambassador, where were you born and raised?

ARMBRUSTER: I was born in El Paso, Texas, at Fort Bliss and mostly raised in Maryland.

We were in Towson, Maryland, Baltimore County, and then Severna Park near Annapolis. Severna Park is on the Chesapeake Bay. One of the early interests I had was in the environment thanks to an 8th grade teacher. She offered us the chance to not just write papers but to go out and do things. She encouraged us to pick an assignment and find a way to get out on the water.

So, I spent the day with a Chesapeake Bay oysterman and interviewed him. I later worked on a charter fishing boat called the *Breezin' Thru*. I got to hear the captain's stories about the Chesapeake when there were just acres and acres of fish. So, from that I developed an environmental awareness. That was a thread throughout my Foreign Service career.

Q: *Now while you were in high school or as a child did you do any traveling either in the U.S. or overseas that sort of began to get you interested in life outside your town?*

ARMBRUSTER: The thing that really grabbed me was reading the *Odyssey* in 7th grade. At first, it seemed really dense and impossible to understand. Our teacher walked us through it so that the classical language became real. Following this epic adventure, ten years in the Trojan War in the *Iliad* for Odysseus and then ten years trying to get home in the *Odyssey* was really a pivotal piece of literature for me in terms of how exciting the world can be and what an adventure it would be to travel.

Gil Callaway and his family were going off to Moscow in 1975. He was the Press Secretary. My mom said, "You have this distant relative you've never met but go help him pack up and move." So I did. They invited me to live with them as a nanny for a year in Moscow. I was 17 and that opened my eyes to what embassy life was like. I played broomball, a hockey game played with a broom, electric tape, and tennis shoes and went to the Marine House and watched movies. Thanks to Gil Callaway and his family I am sitting here talking to you.

———————◇———————

We lived on Vavilova Street, a tram ride from Moscow University. On my first day I remember thinking I had a choice. I could go out, walk around, get lost and explore, or I could wait for people to show me the sites and learn as I go. I walked out and found myself at the Rynok (the market). There, babushkas from Central Asia sold fruits and vegetables, honey, wicker brooms, and recently slaughtered livestock in an open-air bazaar that was a show in itself. I loved it. I soon learned the metro system, hopped on busses to see where they went, and even rode the train beyond the limits to which we were restricted, just to see what would happen. Nothing!

Along with looking after my charges Catherine, Matthew, and Abigail, Gil's wife Susan allowed me to take the open gym teacher job at the Anglo-American school. As a 17-year-old myself, I didn't have much of a curriculum, but I knew how to have fun with a ball, or a puck and we had plenty of cold and ice. I made a glorious $70 a month.

At the embassy I went to the Superbowl and saw the offices just outside the "hardline," the steel vaulted door with a cipher lock on it just like the banks had. Only those with a secret clearance could go through. Intriguing...

One day, Gil said, "Here, wear this camera around your neck. You're a journalist!" I went to Star City, Russia's Cape Canaveral. I saw American astronaut Deke Slayton and the Apollo-Soyuz crew give a presentation to Star City residents. Afterwards, there was a reception at Spaso House, the ambassador's residence, with black caviar that seemed to flow from ice fountains. It was more caviar than I would ever see in my life with the exception of the great barrels of caviar in Yakutia's open-air market. I chatted with the astronauts and cosmonauts and met Alexei Leonov, the first man to walk in space, and had a hint of embassy life. Gil also had parties where he would regale guests with stories of his days as a cowboy, his summer job growing up. I learned that part of being a diplomat is sharing something of yourself.

Red Square was as imposing, ominous, and magical in Soviet days as it is today. The changing of the guard at Lenin's Tomb, the clock's chiming on the hour, and the important looking black Zil limousines coming through the gates gave the Kremlin the sense of power its designers intended.

I was given a tour by Martha Peterson who lived upstairs. She showed me the sights and asked me a lot of questions about the Vietnam War, which had recently ended. I wasn't all that political at that point, but like most Americans, I didn't think the war reflected well on America or helped us geostrategically. It seemed funny she would ask. Later, Martha was expelled from the Soviet Union for being a spy. Apparently not until after she had displayed her martial arts to her KGB watchers. She didn't go down without a fight when she was allegedly caught red-handed at a drop zone with information from the Russian spy she handled. Martha's exploits are featured in the Spy Museum in Washington.

Russian train stations are magical places with a variety of people, families, refugees, criminals, and artists, coming and going 24/7. I went to one *Vokzal,* or station, and happened upon an old woman, all of five feet and 75 pounds...

Dear fellow capitalists, (Mom, Dad, and Brother Chris)

November 16, 1975
Moscow, Russia

Sometimes on my day off I just pick a bus and go. That's what I did today....

I hopped on another bus and was soon in familiar territory... I was at the bottom of the train station escalator when I noticed a woman speaking to me. She was sort of old I guess but not unhealthy. She was pointing at a small suitcase and wanted me to put it on her shoulder. I offered to carry it, but she wouldn't move while I had it, so I put it on her shoulder. It's a wonder she didn't fall over backwards, the thing weighed a ton. If it was filled with iron it wouldn't have weighed more than it did.

It happened that she got on the same train as I did. She sat happily on the suitcase since all the seats were taken. After a few stops she got off. I thought back to how heavy the thing was, and I was feeling sort of guilty for not insisting on carrying it for her before. After a little hesitation I got off the train and offered to carry it for her.

I forget whether or not she argued about it, but if she did it wasn't very strongly. It seemed like we had been walking forever and we were still in the subway station. I had switched the suitcase from my right hand to my left hand and by that time I was carrying it with both arms. She kept trying to tell me things, but I couldn't understand. She wasn't Russian I finally figured out. That doesn't mean she wasn't Soviet; she was just from another part of the USSR.

Finally, we were outside, and she was still trying to tell me something. Like most people she thought if you said something often enough and clearly enough the message would be understood. She told me to hang on a second. I waited with her friend for a few minutes and she returned with a mug. She then pulled out a half of a roll of bread and handed it to me. Then she got a bottle of wine out and poured some in the mug and handed it to me. Both of the women waited anxiously for me to drink. I gritted my teeth not knowing what to expect and took a gulp. They both laughed and told me to turn away from the crowd since it must be illegal to drink in public. The partner had silver teeth. I quickly finished the bread and wine and thanked them very much; they thanked me too and I went on my way.

That outrageously heavy suitcase remains one of life's great unsolved mysteries for me. Tungsten steel? Uranium? I think I'm going to have to go with gold bars. But that kind of experience – when you connect with the local people even if you don't speak the language – stays with you for a long time… maybe forever.

The other thing travel does for you is deepen your historical understanding by putting things in the context of the other country. For example, another Russian mystery for me was where were all the old men? The babushkas drove trucks, chipped ice off the sidewalks, even monitored the men's locker room in the swimming halls, but there were very few old men anywhere. The Soviets' sacrifice of an entire generation in WWII was immediately evident on the street. I did see one vet who wheeled himself around on a homemade trolley. He had lost his legs and yet he moved through the crowd quickly. He somehow caught a tram, swinging himself up on the platform and tucking his trolley under his arm. Churchill's comment that the war was won with British brains, American brawn, and Russian blood is true. The millions of Soviets who lost their lives during the war – an estimated 26 million – and to Stalin's terror – up to a further 20 million – has left a hole in Russia's psyche and a societal trauma through which they are still living. The depths of their suffering in the 20th century are unfathomable for us Americans.

One American at the embassy, Political Officer Larry Napper, gave me an introduction to Russian history. I joined the Callaway family and other embassy folks for a dacha weekend and Larry and I took the embassy rowboat downstream. We came to a forest and decided to park the boat and take a walk. Larry talked about Russia's involvement in WWII in more detail than I had ever heard. I didn't know Churchill's formulation nor how close the Nazis had come to claiming Moscow. He asked if the rowboat would be ok while we hiked. I said, "Sure, there's no crime in the USSR." We got back a half hour later and the embassy rowboat was gone.

It's easy to think of Russia in the Soviet days as dark and dreary, no color. But that's not correct. Cross-country skiing, relaxing at a dacha, taking in the Bolshoi or skating at Gorky Park were all colorful and bright in winter. I was invited to the apartment of a Russian girl once during a snowstorm. We were the only souls on the street one night and caught the tram together. We talked about an art exhibit coming up that weekend and she invited me into her flat. I don't think either of us were interested in the art exhibit. I went up and waited on the steps for a long time while she talked to her mom. But Mom was not about to let an American into her apartment.

The trains were also full of life and connections. I traveled to Leningrad and Helsinki over the Christmas break. Unfortunately, I drank the water in Leningrad and contracted dysentery. I remember when the doctor seemed so concerned saying, "Don't worry doc, you'll give me some pills and fix me right up." He said, "This amoeba stays with you for life." I'm sure I lost a lot of weight and I don't really remember the bout of dysentery itself; it was so severe. The doctor was right, and I admit that like most foreign service officers, my digestion has never been the same and most dairy products are out. So, heed all the medical advice you get when you go overseas. (P.S. something is going to get you anyway sooner or later!)

Little by little my Russian improved. I could read Cyrillic and figure out where the bakeries and restaurants were and read the metro stops. Before I could do that though I would get lost and predictably a babushka would take me out of her way all the way back to the familiar Universitet metro stop. Another babushka let me have it with both barrels for wearing tennis shoes when it was minus 30 outside. I would love to see a calendar featuring super babushkas for every month. They are incredible and still keep Russia going. But I suspect that generation of babushkas in the 1970s, the ones who lived through the war, didn't consider anything a crisis unless it rivaled having the Nazis 15 kilometers away, the city being shelled, and the river iced over at minus 40 degrees. Tough cookies.

November 24, 1975
Dear Truckhousers,

I'll give you the weekend rundown. Sat. night went to a dinner for the principal's (Anglo-American school) anniversary at the British dacha. Sun. morning got a ride into Moscow from the 4th grade teacher, Eddie Morrell. He weighs around 220 lbs. (or 15 ½ stone as they say) and has red hair. In other words, he's a Viking. Eddie gave me a ride to a Russian guy's house who was also at the dacha. That was Andre. Andre invited me up to his apt. while he got his keys. He lives there with his mother on the 10th floor. From his window I could see the TV tower and a few apt buildings and a warehouse or factory, or so I thought. Andre told me it was a prison which is still operating. It was the most dingy, dark, evil-looking building I've ever seen (Lubyanka?). Andre made a couple of phone calls and we were off, pushing the car down the street and recruiting everyone who went by for help.

Finally, we got the car started and he gave me a ride to Gorky Park. I had my skates with me, and they'd frozen the paths over. It was fantastic. Eventually I met up with some Anglo-American students and we played hockey. It was great, I played really well. We played all afternoon and then skated to the other side of the park and got some hot chocolate and pastries...

After the break we all piled into a bus and headed for our respective residences. Most of them lived at Leninsky 83, one street over from Vavilova 83, home of yours truly. I wasn't home for long before Robert Miller, the guy upstairs, called to see if Gil was there. I said no... A few minutes later Robert came down here with two tickets to a theater thing and asked if I'd like to go. Sure! I got my suit on and called Lisa Wold, the general's daughter. Nope she had hepatitis. I'll try Senneca the Finnish girl [I thought]. She said she'd love to. Great, I thought, this is even better.

Senneca speaks English and seemed like a great girl. I'd only met her a couple times. I thought to myself, wait till they hear this, who says I can't arrange things on short notice. It was twenty to six and I told Senneca I'd meet her at the metro by the zoo in 45 minutes or an hour. I dashed out and hopped on a bus, then a trolley, then to the metro and I was right by the zoo. Plenty of time to spare. I waited for around 45 min. And I started wondering if I'd explained the situation well enough. Maybe her English wasn't as good as I thought... I went to the embassy where Senneca lives, not there; back to the metro, nope; back to the embassy. Ah ha! So, what happened was there are two metros by the zoo (I had forgotten about that) and she waited at one and me at the other. Senneca and I have plans to go to Gorky soon. However, it will all be thoroughly arranged first.

OK, you can't relate to that. You have phones with pin drops and "Find My Friends," and all sorts of tools, but in the old days it was easy to get a meet up location mixed up. Easy for me anyway.

The move to Moscow opened my mind to the notion that an international career was possible, even for nannies. Or a "manny" as the other Moscow nannies dubbed me. I liked taking the kids out to the playground, or around the neighborhood for a walk. One afternoon we got caught briefly in a blizzard and had to hole up in another apartment foyer for a while, but luckily it passed quickly, and we were on our way home again.

What else did Moscow teach me? Even though the age of Shackleton and the great pioneering explorers is over, it is still okay to be an explorer yourself. If it's new territory to you, well, that's exploration, and I'm pretty happy when I'm exploring. I had an Australian girlfriend, my first lesson in the joy of international relations, or really just about any relations.

I learned too that it's best to see something through. I left Moscow before my full year was up to travel around Western Europe. I should have stayed to make the most of the experience. The main lesson was that the embassy was filled with regular people. Well, regular smart people and a few eccentrics and playboys – one of the American officers reputedly had every Western stewardess who transited Moscow in his bedroom – but for the most part the diplomats enjoyed playing broomball, they worked hard, and they had kids. They got to go to places like Star City, Spaso House, and the Kremlin as part of their JOB!

And they knew what was behind that steel vaulted door with a cipher lock.

STEP 2 – GET THAT SHEEPSKIN
Westminster, Maryland 1976–1980

College is not a requirement for the Foreign Service. And colleges keep alumni donating by playing on how much you grow during your college years and their nostalgia for young love, sex and discovery – all things that happen to all young people in or out of college. But college is a great delivery system for internships. Internships are the single best way to try a career on for size and see if it fits. And college is a chance to expand your comfort zone. If you are a science nerd, try out for a play. If you want to be a Foreign Service Officer and an ambassador, you are going to have to expand that sweet spot so you can try new food, learn new languages, and lead.

International travel is not a requirement, neither is a foreign language, but a worldview is important. So go to college and join every club that interests you, take every internship you can, and be sure to get good grades, but again, that's not something the examiners have emphasized over the years. (And study abroad. And learn languages.)

Q: *Would you take a second and describe the internship in Annapolis. Was it in the State Legislature?*

ARMBRUSTER: Yes, it was with a state legislator. He was a Democrat and my project was to work on a rails-to-trails pathway. We were able to get that done and it felt really good. He gave me a lot of credit for it. I got to see Steny Hoyer in action. He was the Speaker of the House. He was very impressive. Of course, now he is a national Democratic leader. I would see him occasionally throughout the years on his trips overseas and that was fun.

Q: *You previously mentioned the activities that you had with boating and fishing and so on. This now would have been the late 70s, I guess. There was already some environmental movement by then with pollution in the bay and so on. What were you thinking?*

ARMBRUSTER: The Save the Bay movement was getting started. We would see precipitous drops in some of the fish populations. So, for example, when I was fishing with Captain Harry, we were limited to one rockfish per outing. And we often didn't get that. Then, over the years I saw the rockfish rebound and realized that environmental efforts can pay off. With attention, states can really improve the water quality and the habitat, and the fish can come back. I saw that really dramatically much later in Bikini which suffered from the atomic tests. Bikini came back in quite a big way, with sharks returning to coral reefs. So, nature can come back if we allow it.

Q: While you were majoring in political science did you have a continued interest in environmental activities?

ARMBRUSTER: I did not do well in biology; I can tell you that! They didn't offer an environmental course. I took History and Chinese and Drama. I swam on the swim team for a season, but in terms of environment there really wasn't anything in college that I could sink my teeth into.

Q: It is interesting that you mention drama. There have been other people in the interview who have done drama or public speaking and who look back on that experience as a really helpful tool that would continue to make a difference for them in their career.

ARMBRUSTER: I can imagine, especially for public diplomacy officers. That would make a terrific background. After college I was in journalism for six years. The ability to write quickly is useful. We do a lot of reporting in the Foreign Service, so I was able to tell a story in a cable better because of my journalism experience.

I had a hard time settling into college after Moscow. I wanted to walk to Brazil. I wanted to stay on as mate on Cap'n Harry's fishing boat and have my summer job last forever. Nobody knew the Chesapeake Bay like Harry, captain of the

Breezin' Thru and nobody told stories, jokes, or charmed like Harry Carter of Rock Hall, Maryland. My other summer job was working as waterfront director at Camp Encore/Coda in Sweden, Maine. And I also worked as a Skycap at the airport in Baltimore. And Clement's Hardware store...

I majored in political science, interned at the State Capitol in Annapolis, participated in the Model UN at Harvard, learned to fly on a grass strip runway, swam on the swim team, and spent a semester away from Western Maryland College, now McDaniel at Penn State University. So, even my diverse college experience was not enough to get me into the Foreign Service straight out of college. They were looking for more real-world experience.

STEP 3 – GRAB A PARTNER

The State Department does a good job taking care of "tandem couples." Foreign Service spouses who are both in the State Department. We were not a tandem, but Kathy developed a great international career. I just think it's nice to have somebody with you who understands all your crazy references from around the world. And State today is good for same sex couples, for bringing along an aging parent, and making family situations work if dependents are allowed at post. Some posts are unaccompanied, however, and you can expect to serve at such a post at least once in your career.

Q: OK, so let's go back. As you are approaching the end of your four years in college, did you do any other travel or a year abroad while you were in college.

ARMBRUSTER: I did not. When I got out of college I married Kathy Chandler and for our honeymoon we booked a Yugoslavian freighter and went from Baltimore to Savannah to Casablanca. I think it was my way of telling Kathy, "OK we are going to travel a lot in life!" That was my reintroduction to travel. It was a great trip; we had a lot of fun.

Q: All right you took your honeymoon. What were you two thinking then about the future. Were you thinking about further education or work or…?

ARMBRUSTER: Actually, I realize now that neither of us had a job at the time. We were quite confident we would get a job. So we came back from Morocco and my dad was editing the magazine *Perspectives* at the East-West Center in Hawaii. Kathy and I moved in with my mom and dad. Kathy got her master's in library science and I worked at the University of Hawaii as a communicator with research ships at sea, and then started a journalism career working for Hawaii Public Radio. Then I worked for Nuclear Posture Review (NPR) in Washington, then Maryland Public Television, and then back to Hawaii with the CBS News (Central Broadcasting System) affiliate KGMB-TV.

Q: *So, during that period in Hawaii you were working in radio journalism and maybe some video journalism, TV, and some print as well.*

ARMBRUSTER: Radio and TV. I was a general assignment reporter. But that is where I got back into environmental reporting. There are a lot of great environmental stories in Hawaii. I did a story on Loihi, an undersea volcano. I went with one of the University of Hawaii submarine crews filming that volcanic outflow and the marine life around it. They joked that in 10,000 years there would be hotels and beaches around Loihi. I talked to the entomologists about biodiversity, and evolutionary scientists about island bird life at the University of Hawaii, and astronomy, given Hawaii's telescopes on the Big Island. I produced a regular radio spot on space with one of the university's planetary astronomers. Hawaii was a great place to get back into environmental issues. Then at Maryland Public TV I worked on Farm Day. Environment is also a big issue for farmers. I covered politics and crime and everything else as a general beat reporter, but I did have a specialty in environmental stories. Someone said I had the best job in journalism in Hawaii and I can't disagree.

I don't know how great a prospect I was as a future husband. No award-winning grades, but somehow, I found a beautiful, lifelong, willing, explorer-partner in Kathy Chandler of Westminster, Maryland. She had been to upstate New York and Florida once. She was a local girl and would have been quite happy staying in Westminster. We got married in the backyard of the house we were renting on Main Street. I had the feeling that day that I was making a really good step in life and might be successful after all.

Kathy's dad advised us not to be "too hard on each other." I thought, *what funny advice, we're lovebirds.* But he was right. A little forgiveness, a little keep-that-comment-to yourself goes a long way toward a long marriage.

Being unemployed didn't stop us from taking a Yugoslavian freighter from Baltimore to Casablanca. The honeymoon onboard the boat was great. We learned that not all Yugoslavs get along, that some actually would like to kill each other. I filed that fact away way back in 1980, and sure enough all of the hostility we saw above and below decks onboard the *Tuhobec* played out when Yugoslavia came apart due to ethnic conflict in the 1990s. We crossed the Atlantic with a future New York Times food critic and his girlfriend. We played Scrabble, watched flying fish get out of the boat's way and rocked to the Atlantic swells.

Then we arrived in Casablanca. It sounded romantic. I suffered culture shock. Casablanca's poverty hit me hard. Seeing a homeless young mom breastfeed her baby on the sidewalk was a wakeup call to the realities of a developing country.

Right off the boat we were swindled by a taxi driver who took us all around the city, overcharged us, then dropped us off right across the street, but just out of sight of the dock. Eventually we made our way up to London. Kathy missed her mom and went home, and I went to Italy to visit Gil and family and caught up with Kathy when my money ran out, then we moved to Hawaii.

STEP 4 – FORGET ABOUT THE FOREIGN SERVICE
Honolulu, Hawaii, and Westminster, Maryland 1980–1988

The average age of an incoming Foreign Service Officer is well over thirty. Some diplomats join right out of college, but nowadays that's rare. Many have advanced degrees and professional experience, including military tours. I was thirty. After our European adventure I continued to take the Foreign Service exam. It was sort of a hobby. I failed the written exam the first time, then passed all the sections but was too low on the register to get a call. I think I passed three times. We applied to the Peace Corps and were looking at the Philippines to teach deaf education, but the Peace Corps "lost" our application. The paranoid side of me wondered if my time in Moscow disqualified me from federal service. Of course, they say the Foreign Service is the Peace Corps with air conditioning.

Bigger posts can have over 30 government agencies represented on the country team. In my opinion, the military and the State Department understand each other better than any other two agencies. We are different, but Iraq and Afghanistan have shown us that we need each other in foreign policy. No development is possible without security and no military victory is secured without development. But we do have different missions, different skills, and different cultures. Although there is a lot of mutual respect.

My dad was the editor of *Perspectives* at the East-West Center in Honolulu. We stayed with my parents in Honolulu until Kathy got pregnant and then got kicked out (tough love!) and went to Hardesty Street in Kaimuki, a Chinese neighborhood, where we lived in someone's backyard bungalow. It was cute, cheap, and affordable, especially since I made our bed out of plywood and wooden posts. It was level and sturdy, but not much to look at. Bryan came into the world and my best parenting innovation was taking him outside and hosing him down in his highchair after a meal. You are welcome, new parents!

I virtually camped outside of Hawaii Public Radio's door and wouldn't stop bugging them until they gave me a job gluing egg cartons to the wall for soundproofing. I was their Girl Friday for any odd job. One day there was no one in the recording booth at the top of the hour. So I opened the mic and whispered, "It's five o'clock in the islands."

The general manager called me into his office and said, "OK, this is a radio station, we better figure out a way to put you on the air for real."

So my journalism career was born. I covered everything in Hawaii. Volcanoes, murders, the legislature, Hurricane Iwa. I didn't have the rich, deep voice of Rick Hutto, the voice of Hawaii Public Radio, but for a field guy my voice was fine and I had stories featured on National Public Radio on sumo, domestic violence, and the pesticide heptachlor that was fed to Hawaiian cows until it was found in Hawaiian supermarket milk. That was my first story which aired on NPR. I was in the shower and Kathy said, "Tom! Your story!" I jumped out of the shower, dripping wet, nothing on, and we danced around the bungalow.

Hurricane Iwa hit Kauai hard and I flew to see the damage. A witness said her home had been picked up by a wave and body slammed into the beach. It was gone. A nuclear sub docked at Kauai, provided electrical power from their reactor to local generators. That was national news, so the CBS network guys showed up to interview the Navy captain. We all crammed on a dock to get the interview. I was so squeezed by the media crush I was about to fall into the water. The CBS cameraman grabbed the back of my shirt and held on to me, while filming the scene with his other hand. Once I knew I was going into the Foreign Service a network guy said, "Oh, you're going over to the other side." I never felt like that. I figured we were all on the same side.

Kathy went to the University of Hawaii and got her master's in library science. She got an offer to work in her hometown of Westminster, Maryland. I was happy at Hawaii Public Radio and wanted to stay. Kathy wanted a chance to put her new library skills to work. We flipped a coin. I won. She cried. We moved back. I'd moved a lot in my life. Even now, four years is the longest I've lived anywhere, and when we moved I would miss my friends, but leaving Hawaii was the first time I missed a place like a friend. The ocean breeze, bread and donuts from Kimuraia bakery, the swimming, the air… Hawaii is intoxicating, and we loved it, just like a friend. That love of the ocean never left me. We were at a party not long ago when I overheard Kathy say, "We'll have to leave soon. I have to put my husband in water."

In Maryland, I worked for National Public Radio on *Morning Edition*, getting into work in the wee hours, working with Jean Cochran, Carl Kasell, and Bob Edwards and editing stories and cutting tape. When I had time, I'd do some reporting, including a story on New Zealand's ban of U.S. Navy ships since the navy wouldn't declare which ships had nukes on board. I tried out for a newscaster job and Robert Siegel deemed my voice too high. I could have borrowed a few of the lower register octaves from Rick Hutto. Oh well. It was exhausting working on *Morning Edition* and trying to do freelance feature stories for NPR. I pulled over to sleep one day on the way home and prayed for something full time, something to help me establish a career to support our growing family. Kalia was born in Westminster and I was still day-to-day as needed at NPR. Luckily, they needed me every day for months.

I applied to Maryland Public TV and got a job as a writer on *Farm Day* which prompted Scott Simon to say I was going off to "become a star." And in a way he was right. I soon became a co-host of the show and lo and behold farmers did recognize me! We were on scores of tv stations and it was fun to travel around the country and learn how resourceful America's farmers are. They are smart, savvy businessmen and women.

Hawaii was still calling and when KGMB-TV Honolulu offered me a feature reporter position we moved back. More volcanoes, floods, and more reporting on murder and mayhem. Or, as one of my friends said, "The best job in broadcasting." The stories I really liked were on the environment and science stories; stories about bird evolution on Hawaii, medicine found in coral reefs, and University of Hawaii astronomy discoveries. I also reported on visits to Hawaii by Jimmy Carter and President Reagan. Seeing President Carter and getting to ask him a question was a first for me and I had to think about how to handle it. Should I view this as the new norm, interviewing a president? Or should I be as shell-shocked and excited as I feel about it? Should I learn to be cool? I decided I should be cool, but in retrospect, I think being wide-eyed at it all would have been a better choice. And in truth I was always a little shy around the big celebrities and politicians. I also interviewed Star Trek creator Gene Roddenberry and to this day when the Star Trek credits come on, I say to Kathy, "You know, I once interviewed…" Now I just have to say, "You know…" and Kathy says, "Yes, I know!"

So the next time the selection board had a look at me, I had some travel, and some professional experience, not to mention parenting…

To join the Foreign Service you have to be an American citizen. You can go to careers.state.gov to sign up for the written test and determine which career track you want: political, economic, consular, public diplomacy, or management. You have to be available worldwide to serve at any of the 270 missions around the world. Once you pass the written test, there is a personal narrative, an oral assessment, security and medical clearances, and a suitability review. You have to score well on the "13 Dimensions"; Composure, Cultural Adaptability, Experience and Motivation, Information Integration and Analysis, Initiative and Leadership, Judgment, Objectivity and Integrity, Oral Communication, Planning and Organizing, Resourcefulness, Working with Others, Written Communication, and Quantitative Analysis. They want to know how you'll do in a crisis overseas and how committed you are to public service. How the hell did I ever get in?

STEP 5 – LISTEN TO GEORGE
Honolulu, Hawaii 1988

George was a camp counselor and piano teacher and I was the waterfront director and swim teacher at Camp Encore/Coda. George and I used to sit out on the Adirondack chairs and look up at the Milky Way. I always learned one song every summer to perform. One year it was piano, the next mandolin. But George was a real musician and later a real Boston Brahmin businessman. I took the Foreign Service exam again. Passed again. I was scheduled for the oral in Honolulu so what to wear?

"George, I'm scheduled for the Foreign Service exam on Monday, can I wear my aloha shirt?" If anyone would know it would be my Boston banker friend. Channel 9 gave me a clothing allowance, so I had plenty of colorful Hawaiian shirts.

George said, "Tom, write this down. You need a white shirt, you need a dark suit, you need matching socks and black lace-up shoes. You need a non-offensive tie."

I went shopping.

I took the oral exam in the Federal building. The usual "inbox" questions. You arrive at a post and there are 30 things waiting for you including an impending Congressional delegation and hikers missing in the mountains. What do you do first? You are head of the South Africa Department. How do you deal with apartheid? (Boycott South Africa). Lots of questions, lots of pressure. I passed. Waited. Nothing. Finally, I mentioned to one of Senator Sparky Matsunaga's staffers that I'd taken the test several times, passed, and no offer. He said, "Write Sparky a letter." I did. A few days later I was on the Big Island covering the telescope on Mauna Kea. I was paged in the airport terminal when I landed. Getting paged at the airport in those days meant something big, usually bad. They said to call my wife. Oh, boy. Kathy said the department had called and wanted a call back. Now, the airport page felt like magic.

The Foreign Service is not political. I felt like having passed three or four times I should get an offer. I figured the trip to the Soviet Union was keeping me from getting the call. At that point in the Cold War, it's understandable. Why take a chance? But who knows? Maybe I was too far down the register. In any case, I should have made it a point to stop by Senator Matsunaga's office to say thank you.

Sparky started the U.S. Institute of Peace and he was one of the Fighting 42nd, the most decorated battalion in WWII, made up of Nisei soldiers, proving their American stature with blood. Senator Inouye was another "Go for Broke" soldier who lived and breathed a lifetime of public service.

The registrar called and asked if I would accept an appointment as a management officer. What the heck, I thought? It sounds executive. I forgot that there were political, economic, consular and, these days, public diplomacy officers. Back then, the U.S. Information Agency (USIA) was still independent, that was Gil's agency, and many people asked why, with my news background, I didn't apply to USIA as a public affairs officer. I don't know. I just knew I was given a voucher for a plane ticket for me and my family, and I had to report for duty on June 13.

Back at KGMB I had a fleeting moment of doubt. Not about the career choice so much and that I would be leaving the greatest job in TV, but about Bryan and Kalia. That conflict, between family and career, is at the heart of every assignment decision you make in the Foreign Service. And it doesn't matter whether your kids are small, as ours were, or in college, there will always be questions and sacrifices if you decide to live years of your life abroad. At this juncture our kids were thriving in Hawaii, Kathy was happy as the North Shore bookmobile librarian and Bob Jones in the newsroom had just told me he was going to 'make me a star.' (That again!) The idea of moving on to national news from Hawaii was also appealing, but I still had the Foreign Service dream and it was about to become a reality.

Getting experience outside of government before you join is helpful. It broadens your perspective, gives you some outside contacts, and helps you make sense of other careers. Few people go straight from college into the Foreign Service, so find a job you like and do it for a while and keep in touch with your colleagues when you do join the Foreign Service. Leslie Wilcox, who was a reporter and news anchor and is now president and CEO of Hawaii Public TV, called and she said I did exactly what I set out to do when I left KGMB.

STEP 6 – REPORT TO A-100
Washington, D.C. 1988

So once again we said goodbye to the trade winds, the smells, the food, and the Pacific. And again, it was hard to let go. I learned I had an emotional signature that went with relocating. I would feel a little down about three months before it was time to go, then my brain would focus on the next post and I'd be ready to move when it was wheels-up time.

There wasn't much time to miss Hawaii. A-100 is bootcamp for diplomats. These days there is also a "Crash and Bang" course that is open to everyone, including spouses, which is mandatory if you are going to a high threat post for over 45 days. I took it recently to get ready for an inspection of Embassy Chad and Embassy Mauritania. In Crash and Bang you learn emergency procedures, evasive driving, surveillance detection, emergency medical protocols including tourniquet techniques, and how to recognize an AK-47 from an AR15. It's a fun week-long course but they've taken the shooting training out. Too bad.

Q: OK, 1988 and your wife is OK with this and you talked about it and she realizes you are going to be moving around a little bit.

ARMBRUSTER: Kathy has known for a long time that this was something I wanted. She has been very successful as a librarian in libraries all over the world and has wondered whether all this disparate experience really adds up to anything? We went back to New York years later and within a week she had a job offer from a really prestigious school. I think international experience is valuable in any profession. It was a good gamble for us.

Q: Describe your class as well as you can remember.

ARMBRUSTER: We were about 30-some A-100 classmates. Our median age was 30. Some people had advanced degrees but not many. We had some prior military and we had one former Marine. In fact, he gave us a great tour of Gettysburg which was really memorable, and he was selected as the outstanding classmate. The gender balance was not 50-50; predominantly male. We had at least one person with Asian ethnicity and a black man, but not terribly diverse otherwise.

Q: And the experience of A-100 [that] sometimes people stay in touch for years later. Did that work for you?

ARMBRUSTER: Yes, although I was voted the classmate least likely to be seen in Washington. I only did one tour in Washington. So, I didn't make it to the reunions, but I did keep in touch with classmates via email. That has grown to be a powerful thing for people to have a terrific network and grapevine. So, people know before going to a post everybody's reputation. It is a very positive development.

In A-100 you learn about the state department culture, hear war stories from old Foreign

Service officers, and bond with your class. Reagan was president and George Schultz was

Secretary of State, or SecState, or simply "S." There was a great story circulating about Schultz. Not only did he go down to the cafeteria and eat with the troops, he also reportedly would call outgoing ambassadors into his office. He would chat, then point to the big globe that stood on a pedestal in his office and say, "Show me your country."

The ambassador would look at the globe, gently move it around to the right hemisphere and say "Ghana," or "Uruguay," or "Burma."

Schultz would shake his head, spin the globe and land his finger on America. "That's your country, ambassador. Don't you forget it. Have a good tour."

We weren't sworn in by Secretary Schultz. As I recall, it was done quickly by one of our instructors. We raised our right hands, and I said:

I, Thomas H. Armbruster, do solemnly swear that I will support and defend the Constitution of the United States against all enemies, foreign and domestic, that I will bear true faith and allegiance to the same, that I take this obligation freely, without any mental reservation or purpose of evasion, and I will well and faithfully discharge the duties of the office on which I am about to enter. So help me God.

A-100's best day is Flag Day. That's the day they call you up in a big auditorium with a lot of dignitaries and families in attendance and hand you a flag. Hopefully you know it, because that's where you are going. I was handed a blue flag with a white cross. Finland. Great assignment. I learned later that the job was supposed to go to a more seasoned officer who had already been tenured, but he had been sent elsewhere. My boss, Stuart Spoede, said he would only accept a junior officer if he could get the "pick of the litter" from A-100. A-100 decided I was it. We were given our black, diplomatic passports, along with our orders, able to wrangle out of our lease thanks to a military and diplomatic assignment clause; our friends walked us to the gate at Baltimore-Washington International Airport (BWI) and we took off for Helsinki.

Flag Day 1988

STEP 7 – DO YOUR FIRST TOUR
Helsinki, Finland 1988–1990

Getting out of the embassy van we had our first international incident. Before I could even get out, Bryan had hit the ground, made a snowball, and threw it at the driver. He nailed him. I held my breath. Aki laughed and I breathed a sigh of relief. Diplomatic crisis averted. I remember Aki for that and for playing Level 42's new cassette in the embassy van for the next two years. It was his one and only cassette and he loved it.

Our house was a nice black and white functional townhouse that led to the water in the backyard.

I was Deputy Director of the Soviet Support Office. Sounds very grand, but the reality was

I helped to run a warehouse – well, two warehouses, one classified, one "unclass" – to supply Embassy Moscow and Embassy Leningrad with everything from pencils to armored cars. I also bought their supplies with the help of Jaana, Rauno, Aki, Virpi, and Blue and we made sure they got what they needed on time. I bought millions of dollars' worth of equipment.

We communicated by telex and then, a miracle, by fax. We also traveled regularly to

Moscow and Leningrad to check the inventories of government furniture in American homes. Most of the Non-expendable Property Application (NEPA) tags were in the top drawer of dressers, so our guys inadvertently knew just about everybody's favorite birth control.

Getting to know the Finns took a while. First, learning how they stood up to the Soviets, twice in WWII, fighting them on skis, with General Mannerheim outsmarting them with a fraction of their forces. One of the films about the Winter War showed a Finn dropping his farm tools, picking up his rifle and heading to the front when he got word it was war without any word to his family. Quintessentially Finnish.

I was told I would also rotate through the other sections, political, econ, and consular. Helsinki was a Cold War hotbed of spies. The Deputy Chief of Mission (DCM), though, played up the importance of old-fashioned Foreign Service reporting. He said, "Information that you pay for is not any better than information you get the old-fashioned way, interviewing people on the street, listening and analyzing." Good advice.

In the political section I was able to do some reporting on the effects of the Chernobyl accident on Finnish wildlife, particularly reindeer. I interviewed the experts and enjoyed putting my old journalism skills to work. The department wasn't that impressed with my writing though. In A-100 one of the instructors had said, "You're good, you write well, but everybody writes well. You need to craft every paragraph. You need to up your game and not think that you can just get by because you can write fast." More good advice.

My first chance to get information the old-fashioned way and report on a more burning issue was a trip to the Baltics. The Soviet Union was just on the edge of falling apart and the

department was desperate for reports. I went to Riga and joined a political officer from

Leningrad. At one point he had another meeting and I was on my own in the town square. Latvian flags, rather than Soviet hammer and sickle flags, were flying everywhere. The square was full of protesters, on all sides. There were old Soviets haranguing young revolutionaries, but the generational divide wasn't 100 percent. I started asking, discreetly, what they were saying as the two sides were debating hotly in the square. In no time the crowd discovered that I was American.

Suddenly all the hopes of pro-independence people and all the anger of the pro-Soviet people was directed at me. I felt the full weight of "representing America" then and there. They wanted answers. They wanted support, even moral support. I realized all that America represented to them and I never forgot the weight of that expectation from the crowd. When America lends support to an oppressed people it resonates. For years we had not recognized the annexation of the Baltics into the USSR. Now that stood for something.

The crowd eventually began dispersing and an elderly man took my arm. 'Come with me,' he said. He wasn't threatening. Far from it. The friend or foe algorithm said loudly "friend" and I followed him. He lived in a little basement space. Apartment would be too grand a word. He opened a can of meat, what I'll never know, but we shared it with some crackers. Through his broken English and my primitive Russian we communicated. Finally, he went to a cupboard and found some photos. This was why he had picked me out. I don't know if he hoped the photos would go to the press or just to the U.S. government.

From Riga we went back to Leningrad where I was hit by a violent illness. I could hardly stand, and the dizziness hit me so hard it felt as though the room had tipped sideways. The embassy sent a Russian doctor who did not seem too surprised by the symptoms and prescribed a suppository. I got better fast, but I always wondered if that was the KGB reminding me that I was on their turf. It wasn't the last time I would be sent a message. I put the photos in the classified diplomatic pouch when I got back to Helsinki and the department's Intelligence and Research Department sent a heartfelt thank you.

Later in the tour, I picked up more intel. It was at a hockey game. The Soviet diplomats and American diplomats played against the Finnish Foreign Ministry. We were outfitted with pads, uniforms, and helmets. I played a good while and scored a goal. One of two or three versus the Finns' roughly 20 goals. The Finns played hard, checking, slashing, and giving us no quarter.

In the locker room one of the Soviets waited until he could say something to me privately. He said, "Moscow is going to do something tomorrow." I said thank you. I didn't know what to do with the information. It was late and everyone had gone home. I couldn't call the DCM because I didn't want anyone listening to know that the Soviet had given me information. Plus, what did he mean? Moscow could be doing anything! I could have driven to the DCM's house... but, I didn't. The next day tanks went into Riga and it was the bloodiest day of a mostly bloodless fall of an empire. I learned the lesson. If you see something, or hear something, say something. When I saw someone photographing the embassy in Moscow on a TDY (temporary duty) trip there I immediately told the Regional Security Officer. I had learned the lesson.

Presidential visits are a big part of embassy life as are Congressional delegations, or

CODELs. Everybody complains about them. I love them. In Helsinki, it was President Bush coming to talk with Gorbachev about a new world order. We had very little time to prepare. Just so you don't get the wrong idea, I wasn't asked to the strategy sessions about how Russia could reintegrate into the Western world. My job, as a junior officer, was handling baggage. Kathy was also working as this was an "all hands-on deck" event but she came down with a migraine and "curtailed."

The best part of the presidential visit was the embassy meet and greet. They had everyone in a group getting organized for a photo. Bryan was packed in with the rest of the embassy community. He was eight or nine and kept saying, "When is the president going to get here? Where is the Prez?" President Bush turned around and smiled and said, "Oh, he's here. Don't worry." Of course, Bryan is also famous for exclaiming to Mrs. Wetzel one day when she seemed perturbed, "Loosen your bra Mrs. Wetzel," using the golfing adage my father often used when a player left a putt short. It seemed appropriate to Bryan, and he thought he used the phrase exactly as his grandfather would have. This was all explained to the principal after the call home.

Meanwhile, back at the embassy meet and greet, Kalia was out of sorts because the press corps ate all the cookies. President Bush, ever gracious, also stopped by to comfort her!

She had been going to Finnish daycare and was inventing a Finnish language of her own, with all the right cadence and many of the right words. High diplomacy was not much fun for her at age four.

Kalia was also a hero one day when it was minus ten. Kathy went outside briefly and got locked out. Kalia was reading on the couch. Kathy tapped on the window and said, "Honey, let Mommy in the front door." Kalia jumped up, went to the front door and tried to open it. After a few minutes she got tired and went back to read her book on the couch. "Kalia, you need to try really, really hard for Mommy!" Kalia went back at it and finally got the door open. Kathy's still grateful for that!

I had a chance to go out to Air Force One to grab a bag they needed in town. I still have the pack of Air Force One playing cards somewhere! An added bonus of the presidential visit for me was getting to know the White House communications guys who let me make a call anywhere in the world for free. Hello Mom! This was long before Skype and back when an international call cost some serious bucks. And bucks were something that was in short supply. A trip to McDonald's was almost out of the question. Finland is still expensive. But cross-country skiing is free, public transportation is cheap and available, and as our embassy cashier once told me when I complained about the size of my paycheck, "Oh Tom, it's only money. It just goes round and round." Yep, round and round with none of it sticking to our fingers!

I worked on many high-level visits over the years, and the excitement and adrenaline is always there, but that first visit of President Bush to Helsinki was special. Not to mention Alice Cooper. Presidential visits are great for morale and they are also a chance for "deliverables" and to move the ball forward. The enormous amount of time spent choreographing these short visits makes sense because they are so short and have to run perfectly. They make a lasting impression in the country and may be the only presidential visit for decades. Every embassy officer is responsible for making sure they go off without a hitch. I guess we did well since I, along with the warehouse guys, earned a Superior Honor Award for that trip, my first.

But mostly I was dedicated to being deputy director at the warehouse. I enjoyed the work and Stuart was a great mentor. He helped me figure out how to deal with the demands from Embassy Moscow and the admin officer in Helsinki. Stuart seemed to know everything and everyone. He was a Texan and he and his family took us in as friends. One of the realities of Foreign Service life hit me when Stuart received a call that his mother had died. Here he was thousands of miles away. We could hear him through the thin warehouse walls crying. The staff, normally outgoing and playful, were quiet, respectful, and caring. If there was anything we could have done for Stuart in addition to offering kind words we would have. Life happens when you are away.

Q: *Did you get training in Finnish?*

ARMBRUSTER: I did not. Kathy did. She took advantage of that so she was our spokesperson when we went out in the world and would buy us goodies.

Q: *So, since you had somebody in your family to handle the day-to-day speaking, I imagine all the Finns you worked with spoke English.*

ARMBRUSTER: They did. I did learn to count. *Uxi, koksi, kolmi...* We still have Finnish friends. I took some Finnish while I was there and learned enough Finnish to get around. It is a very difficult language. I can say the black cat is on the table. *Musta kissa on podella.* More importantly we learned the Finnish culture. We have a sauna at home now in Ithaca, New York. I really enjoyed working with the Finns; they were professional and they certainly know the Russians better than anybody. Once you make friends with a Finn, you are friends for life.

———

Of course, making friends is not always easy. Kathy was eager to use her Finnish and on her first walk in the neighborhood in Helsinki she saw a woman coming her way along the path. Nice opportunity she thought.

Kathy said, "*Hyyva paiva!* Good afternoon!"

The well-dressed Finnish woman drew herself up, looked Kathy up and down and said in perfect English, "But I don't even know you."

Kathy managed to say, "I just wanted to say hello."

The woman considered, finally nodded curtly, said, "Hello!" and walked on.

Well, in the end we have Finnish friends that we consider family. Once you are in the club, you are in! Finns are wonderful people, if somewhat reserved. One of the favorite jokes they tell about themselves goes like this:

Ole the Finn and Sven the Swede went fishing.

Every morning, Sven boomed out, "Good morning Ole!" And then they fished in silence the rest of the day.

One day, Sven began saying "Good morning..." and Ole shot him.

The police came and said, "Why did you kill him?"

Ole said, "He talked too much." Ah.

Note to colleges: Don't let freshmen "test out" of a language. I tested out of Spanish in college when I should have doubled down. Find ways to incentivize languages, at least for international relations students. Language proficiency is the single biggest determinant of morale and effectiveness in an embassy. *Pravda*!

Stuart introduced me to kayaking and camping in Finnish lakes and was a model for what we now call "work-life balance." He worked hard, but weekends were family time.

Several years later when Stuart was back in Washington overseeing building projects like the new embassy in Moscow, he found himself bumping into the wall and falling frequently. He was diagnosed with brain cancer. We got to see him shortly before surgery. Stuart didn't talk about his illness. He didn't make it.

He had worked at Embassy Moscow, and like everyone who ever worked there, including me, he was exposed to microwave radiation that the Soviets and Russians still beam at the embassy. Whether that was a health risk or not, I don't know. The loss of Stuart as a friend and mentor was a big one for me; it was a big loss for the State Department, particularly in the management ranks; and a devastating loss for his family. I was happy to attend the ceremony naming a building on the Moscow embassy compound in his honor, the Spoede Building.

When you are in the Foreign Service, it helps if you can get inspiration from a variety of faiths. We've been Anglicans, Lutherans, Methodists – pretty much whichever church has a service in English is a pretty good candidate to be our church. I'd also be happy to be a part-time Buddhist. I'm not dogmatic.

I figure God put in place an incredible universe. It works on the atomic level, where we don't really get to play except in the particle accelerator labs. And then there's the galactic level, where we are too tiny to play; but at our level, there is a lot we can do. And we are responsible for it. And that's ok. Some say if God really loved us He wouldn't allow for bad things to happen. I don't buy it. We have free agency, the greatest gift of all. And we can learn throughout our lifetimes. The Bible has wonderful passages that sustain us travelers.

I rely on:

> *Go out into the World in Peace*
> *Be Brave*
> *Keep Hold of What is Good*
> *Never Pay Back Wrong for Wrong*
> *Support the Weak and Distressed*
> *Give Due Honor to Everyone*
> *Be Always Joyful*
> *Pray Continuously*
> *Give Thanks Whatever Happens*
> *For This is What God in Christ Wills for You*[1]

And

> *Trust in the Lord*
> *With all your Heart*
> *And lean not on your understanding*
> *In all your ways*
> *Acknowledge Him*
> *And He Shall Direct your Path*[2]

---

[1] 1 Thessalonians 5.
[2] Proverbs 3: 5-6.

And

God did not give us a spirit of fear
But of power, love, and understanding[3]

Ok, I hope he's watching and maybe keeps a look out for us, or whispers to us every now and then, but all in all I think it is up to us to use the resources we've been given. And if traveling around the world has taught me anything it is that the world is an incredibly rich place. Nature can bounce back if we let it. Even Bikini, the site of multiple nuclear tests, is teeming with life. Our planet has sustained life for billions of years, and if we don't screw it up it will continue to for billions more.

In Helsinki we used to attend services at the beautiful Anglican church in the downtown square. There, we met the Websters. Di, an internationally acclaimed author, her son Johnny, now a documentary filmmaker; Anu, at the time Johnny's beautiful Finnish girlfriend and soon to be wife, and Spratty, Di's daughter and a talented emergency room doctor. And I should take this opportunity to thank Johnny for saving my life with the Heimlich maneuver during a Christmas dinner. Thank you, Johnny!

Johnny and I bonded in my tandem kayak, often getting soaked and ending up in a Finnish restaurant laughing and dripping as we changed into dry clothes.

We traveled with Johnny and Anu to Moscow by train, and from there to Zagorsk, one of the historic sites of Russia's Orthodox church. With the Soviet Union breaking up, the mood in Moscow at that time was lighter, more open. Our taxi driver regaled us, just as a New York cabbie would, with his view of the world and the politicians in Moscow. He had nicknames for everyone – Gorby, Shevvy – he was a riot, until we got to Zagorsk and he asked for his $50 dollars. I insisted that we had agreed on $15 dollars. Our cabbie went into a classic Russian funk, sulking at the restaurant and refusing to talk to us. Finally, he seemed to come to a decision, stormed out, and came back smiling. "Bad news. Someone slashed my tires. Now you have to pay to fix it to go home!" Hmmm.

---

[3]   2 Timothy 1: 7.

"Well," I said, "I used to live in Moscow, and I know there is a train station right over the hill and I think we'll just wander over there and catch the train."

Helsinki was great for skating, cross-country skiing, and especially kayaking. I bought a

German made tandem kayak and spent hours on the Gulf of Finland. Sometimes I would get out to the big swells, far out to sea with the land just visible behind me. It was a good thing I

was training.

I was invited to join a team of Finns paddling from Helsinki to Tallinn, still in the USSR, in midsummer 1989. The trip took us 23 hours of pure paddling. My partner from the embassy, Juuka, was a strong paddler. We surfed the swells, saw a sea lion, and were at our limit when we arrived in Tallinn. Along the shore we passed what looked like military barracks and heard a man singing drunkenly, but beautifully. There was a huge clock in the port and our goal was in sight. As we pulled in, I gave a rebel yell. Juuka's reserved Finnish soul was mightily offended, but it felt good to me. A Soviet border guard checked my American diplomatic passport and almost fell over laughing. After that, there was a brief ceremony on shore with local officials, we all piled into a sauna, and I promptly fell asleep. The trip back was aboard a ferry with our kayaks lined up on deck. We each got a medal for the two-day trip and I like knowing that I am the only American diplomat to ever arrive in the Soviet Union by kayak. Whenever I talk to a group of university students that is always the first thing they ask about. I wish we were forced to fend off pirates or saw mermaids or something, because really it was just a long, hard paddle.

We had some nice family adventures in the kayak too, putting the kayak on the roof of our car and loading it onto a train that went to the Arctic circle. From there we paddled in Hammerfest and northern Norway and caught Arctic char to eat over a campfire. Kalia used to fall asleep in the front seat of the kayak. Some kids you put in a stroller; some nap better in a rocking two-man kayak.

My friend Fred Smyth came to Finland and we arranged for a ride in a Soviet icebreaker. They let us don dry suits and bob around in the Gulf of Bothnia. It all confirmed what I thought; the Foreign Service is going to be a great adventure. After all, that's why I joined.

In those days before the internet people did crazy things. Fred and I played Scrabble by mail. We drew the board, complete with double word and triple word tiles and each set up a board at home. Fred would make a move, write it on our game board on paper, send me news from home and mail it off. I'd do the same. It took us about a year to play one game. I can't remember who won, but that probably means Fred. We were incredibly competitive. In fact, I asked Kathy out on a date because I wanted to beat Fred to the punch. They were in a play together in college and Kathy appeared in one scene in her bra. That was pretty risqué for a small, previously Methodist, college in Maryland.

I could feel the sands of the hourglass running out in Finland. They had a goodbye for us with a picnic on the water. I could tell the guys were up to something when we were standing on a pier and I felt surrounded. Sure enough, they planned to throw me in the water as a last goodbye. I said, "Ok, ok, just let me take my wallet out." I didn't have a wallet, but I put my hand in my pocket, lowered my head and took a few guys overboard with me.

Finland had a lifelong impression on me. I can still picture our row house on Kulosaari; the hill that went down to the water that we would sled down in winter; seeing the aurora from our bedroom window and getting the kids up to see it. And we still use Finnish expressions. Well, maybe not exactly Finnish, but the English phrase we would hear from the shopkeeper at the local market, "Like you, Finnish goodies?" We did! All the things I still wanted to do and places to go and the time was going. We did get out to a wooden cabin on a lake a few times and that is still one of the most peaceful scenes anywhere in the world in my mind. No wonder the Finns are the happiest people on Earth.

STEP 8 – GET OFF PROBATION
Washington, D.C. 1990–1991

Finland was a "directed assignment." The folks in A-100 figure out who to send where. After that, when I joined, it was every man for him or herself. Look at the bid list, lobby, hope your "corridor reputation" is good and give it your best shot, just as you would a real job.

Stuart urged me to go from Helsinki to a new mission in Kiev for my onward assignment, but I had already been selected for Havana. At a recruiting session in the Department an officer said the requirement to get a job at the U.S. Interests Section in Cuba was the "ability to fog a mirror." *I can do that!* I thought. Since I had accepted the job it would be poor form to take the more responsible job Stuart had lined up for me in Ukraine, a freshly minted independent country. I had also considered Chiang Mai, Thailand but the DCM didn't think that would be a good post for young kids. Now I know things happen. If something better comes along, take it. No hard feelings, nothing personal.

These posts are from an actual bid list, mostly with transfer dates of 2015, but some 2017 for language.

Have a look and choose your top three posts:

Brussels

Manila

Tokyo

Seoul

Kabul

Tunis

London

Cairo

Bogota

Erbil

Remember, you have to be available worldwide. You can't exclude any post in the world. If you chose London, Tokyo, and Brussels, you are probably joining

41

the Foreign Service for different reasons than I. For many people, the idea is to limit your time at hardship posts and maximize your time in London, Paris, and Rome. I figured I could go there anytime as a tourist, but the hardship posts were only likely to be experienced through the Foreign Service. If Tunis, Bogota, and Kabul have your imagination going, then you'll know how I felt every bid season – like a kid in a candy store. You're going to pay me to learn a language and travel to these places? Oh my.

But it is more complicated than just picking the most exotic spot. I usually did a spreadsheet that considered these factors: Schools for the kids, the job for me, prospects for Kathy, sports and recreation opportunities, money, career, language, and intangibles. I'd give each category a score from zero to ten. Kabul would get a ten for money, London a two, as I figured it would be expensive, but Kathy would probably be able to work. When the kids are young, schools drive the process. After that, who you know, what you like, and the "needs of the service."

To continue in the State Department you have to get off of "language proba-tion." There are various incentives to learn languages too, both in terms of promotion and pay. My two languages are Spanish and Russian. I obtained a 3+/3 in Spanish, with zero being no proficiency and five being a native speaker, so I got off probation. I missed adding a plus to my reading score by not figur-ing out that *tentación* equals temptation. The tester was exasperated with me too… are you sure you can't figure that out? Nope! My brain refused to budge. I guess I could just fog a mirror.

Our Spanish group was small, just four people or so. After six months in the same room, you get to know each other pretty well. I nicknamed our group the *Pingüinos*, my favorite Spanish word. I'll let you figure out what it means!

Every Foreign Service family develops their own language. I can see why languages are constantly evolving and adopting new words. If you are ever on the border and experience Spanglish, you'll know that languages are as fluid as water. "*Yo voy al supermarket para popcorn and pretzels, then nos vemos!*" Accept-able border talk. For the Armbruster family the lexicon includes, "Are you *pau* with that?" (Are you *done* with that?) The Hawaiian word *pau* just works so nicely. And the Russian *za chem!* Or *for what!* Your brain often just reaches for the first foreign word it remembers when trying to recall a word. A Russian word might appear first, then the brain says nope, and the Spanish word finally comes. When you start dreaming in the language you are learning you are on your way. Languages do enrich your soul. I feel a little more opinionated in Russian than English. When you get language training throw yourself into it; you'll plateau at some, but you have to just keep at it. There is no language app in the world that will get you where you need to be in three weeks. You are not stupid; it just takes a long time.

Russian, learned years after I first visited Moscow, started with me entering the program with a zero plus, I still had a few words and could read Cyrillic. The Foreign Service Institute (FSI) teachers are all native speakers and they are excellent. They know how to get us to speak, when all our instincts say, "shut up until you can get it right!" They make us speak like babies, then kids, and finally like diplomats. Of course, I can negotiate a nuclear arms treaty, but I would have trouble getting all the right stuff on my pizza. The FSI teachers focus on the language you will need to get the job done. They also offer language training to spouses. Kathy took Finnish, Spanish, Tajiki, and Russian and she was often our lead linguist on family trips.

STEP 9 – DO YOUR CONSULAR TOUR
Havana, Cuba 1991–1993

Watching Cubans expertly roll handmade cigars was one of the many pleasures of our tour in Havana from 1991 to 1993. Scuba diving, hiking to the wonderful Soroa waterfall with an orchid farm at the start of the trail, biking the countryside on deserted highways, and visiting remote towns with artifacts purportedly from Christopher Columbus himself, were also highlights.

Flights were so infrequent that the Interests Section didn't know at which airport we were arriving and so we missed the van and took a taxi to the embassy. With no formal diplomatic relations, the American presence was officially under the Swiss flag and was known as the U.S. Interests Section. I argued I should get home leave in Zurich, but that never worked. It was a diplomatic fig leaf. I saw the Swiss ambassador once. In most ways we functioned just like an embassy. Except, the principal officer could not meet with Fidel. Soon enough we were ensconced in *Quinta Avenida*, a former mafioso home, we imagined, judging by the horseshoe decoration on the patio. It was lush, with lime, papaya, and mango trees.

I saw Fidel twice. First at the Pan Am games. The stadium was packed, and Fidel and his entourage were in an upper tier of the stadium. Spontaneously, it seemed, fans started a wave with sections of hundreds rising to their feet. On the first wave people stood up threw their hands back and cheered. Fidel jumped up on the first wave. Most of his entourage stayed seated. On the second go-round everyone in his crew leaped up. The man had charisma.

The games were great and the level of baseball incredible. Former Yankees owner George

Steinbrenner sat right in front of us watching the U.S. vs. Cuba game. We all marveled at a Cuban double play where the shortstop didn't even glove a grounder, he just batted it to the second baseman with the back of his glove. The second baseman barehanded the ball and neatly turned the play. And they were so cool about it. No celebrations, just cool professionalism and Cuban flair. Steinbrenner gave Kalia a Yankees cap with the autograph, "My Yankees Love You," and Bryan got one that read "Future Yankee."

The second time I saw Fidel was at the Marina Hemingway where adventurer Thor

Heyerdahl arrived by boat. Fidel was close enough to touch and again he radiated charm.

One of my friends, Lisa Bobbie Schreiber Hughes, a future ambassador herself and then the General Services Officer, translated for Fidel. Show me another profession where opportunities like that come up.

Translating is a big job. I met the interpreter who worked for Reagan during the Reykjavik meeting with Gorbachev. He couldn't sleep the night before the big summit, until he finally told himself that in the scheme of things, in the universe, maybe the meeting was not such a big deal. The stakes weren't quite so high for Lisa Bobbie, but it was a memorable, once in a lifetime event.

We were lucky. The requirement that diplomats submit a diplomatic note for travel outside Havana was not in effect, so we went everywhere except Guantanamo – at least everywhere we could get to on half a tank of gas. We never knew if we'd find gas once we got outside of the capital. That was during the "Special Period in a Time of Peace." Translation: It was a tough time given the end of the Soviet subsidies. In the early 90s people were really struggling. We had thousands of Cuban applicants for visas and we mainly had to say "No." One young man told me that if I turned him down for a visa, he was getting onto an inner tube and floating to Florida. He said if he died on the way it was on me. Nice try! Another family made their escape when a small plane from Florida landed on a lonely road and they jumped in and made the trip back to Florida safely.

Not long after our tour the *Hermanos al Rescate* private plane was shot down by the Cuban Air Force. That cut short a "dissent cable" that I wrote with two of my Interests Section colleagues. We felt the U.S. would benefit from opening up with Cuba. Business would benefit. Tourists would benefit. And maybe we could learn something from them too.

Cubans have always been inventive and given a chance will flourish. Who else could keep Hudsons and DeSotos running for so long? And Cuba was no longer exporting revolution. But the idea of rapprochement after the shoot-down seemed out of the question and we withdrew the dissent cable. In retrospect, we should have gone ahead, some battles are worth fighting, even if you know you are going to lose.

The Cubans were naturally curious about foreigners. When people asked where I came from, I would say, "Guess!" Poland, Russia, Germany, were a few of the guesses, but I said, "*No, mucho mas cerca!*" (No, a lot closer!) Americans were rare in those days. Informal contact by Cuban citizens with Americans could lead to reprisals, so most were wary. And the U.S. had its own restrictions and reporting requirements on diplomats. I've always said Kathy's "no contact policy" was a lot stricter than the State Department's. But we made one great friend: Hiram. Hiram was a master equestrian. We visited him and his horses at Luna Park on Sundays. He trained the Cuban national team, had terrific horses, and because he had traveled internationally and was a well-known sportsman, he felt safe enough to invite us into his home. It was an honor and another treasured memory.

Although he had traveled to some international equestrian competitions, Hiram had very little contact with Americans. He said, "You're not like the Americans in movies. You don't smoke; don't drink; don't swear!" Cuban TV showed the most violent, awful American movies around, and I did not fit the stereotype!

The U.S. attempts to broadcast more favorable tv and radio were largely blocked by Cuba. We were thrilled once to see *Jeopardy* somehow drift over the airwaves from Florida and onto our set!

Another friend was Lilya, the language teacher. She was as old as a DeSoto herself and remembered the Cuban Missile Crisis. Every night during that tense time she and her family went out to dinner, figuring that each night could be their last. I guess they got news on an AM radio or maybe Lilya's family was in government and knew the situation. In any case, they knew that the missiles that the Soviets had installed couldn't stand and that war was a hair trigger away.

Bryan took all of 5th grade in Spanish, so he took to Hiram's teaching quickly. Bryan even competed in a horseback competition in Florida on our home leave and came away with a ribbon. Kalia's great pastime was playing with a wooden plank in the backyard. Where that plank took her in her imagination one can only guess!

We also went to a park to see the Boxer Club in action. On Sundays I'd take the kids to the park and watch the boxers work out. We ended up taking home a puppy named "Luna." Luna became "Chessie," and Chessie traveled with us from Cuba to the U.S., Russia, and Mexico. We were lucky to find a Cuban trainer who taught Chessie to go into her kennel on her own, an invaluable skill for a Foreign Service pet. Chessie also let any embassy workmen come in unhindered, another plus in a profession where people come and go into your house all the time. Chessie's only rule was that no one could leave the car before I did. If you tried, she'd try and keep you in. Once everyone knew the rules it was fine.

While tourists in those days were scarce, there were a few American prisoners during our tour. I visited, brought magazines and news from the States, and tried to get a sense of the prisoner's conditions and report any mistreatment. One American had hijacked a plane and had expected to be welcomed into the Cuban revolution with open arms. It was not working as well as he had planned. I visited him and he still seemed to be waiting for the Cubans to recognize that he was a fellow revolutionary, instead of an international criminal.

Here is a little bit about his story from the Washington Post:

William Potts. One of the last hijackers and another Black Panther Party militant, Potts became known somewhat mockingly as "the homesick hijacker." Potts diverted a commercial flight from New York City to Cuba in 1984, hoping to go on to South Africa to join the antiapartheid movement. He was imprisoned for 13 years and then lived as a political exile. In 2013, he returned to the United States and earlier this year pleaded guilty to kidnapping. He is now in prison and eligible for parole in 2021.

Robert Vesco, on the run for financial crimes in the U.S. and known to be a big contributor to President Nixon in his re-election campaign,[4] was another American in exile who would show up at the International School every now and then. But for the most part, there were very, very few Americans in a country that rich New Yorkers used to fly to for lunch.

One of my first work challenges was to reduce the backlog of visa interviews. I was the Nonimmigrant Visa Chief, so my job was to have our team interview as many people as possible. Castro decided cleverly that he didn't need to keep Cubans from leaving. The U.S.

government said 'no' to most applicants anyway. Let us be the bad guys. We could each interview up to 120 people a day. Everyone wanted to go to Florida, and we had to decide who was telling the truth when they said they planned to come home after a short stay in the U.S.

Shrewdly, the Cuban government was not shy about letting us know how they felt about us either. We went to a circus, the whole family, and returned to the car only to find dog shit had been put under the door handles. That was really incomprehensible and shocking for Bryan. Worse was to follow. I went on a trip out of town to check on people who had returned to Cuba from the U.S. under a humanitarian program. When I returned to my hotel room, I found the bathroom sink filled with blood.

The harassment and being followed didn't bother me. Sometimes it was funny, like when a team of Cuban spies bent on following us came right along into a sugarcane field when we got lost. They all looked the other way as if they were bird-watching or something.

I went scuba diving for the first time in Cuba. My dive masters were former Cuban special forces guys. We were about 100 feet down when I realized I had no idea what I was doing or what I would do in an emergency. I decided I would get some lessons before scuba diving again.

---

[4]   https://www.nytimes.com/2008/05/09/world/americas/09vesco.html

Another adventure was being sent to Miami with $15,000 in cash. The embassy had been flooded by a deluge from the sea. Papers and personal treasures left by panicked Cubans before the revolution were in the Interests Section basement and suffered some damage. This was no hurricane, just a king tide. There were no deaths from the flood, but people were trapped in buildings until the water subsided.

I had three days to buy all the supplies I could and bring them back. I spent the money, got it to the plane and came home and promptly passed out from lack of sleep. I tried to rally and go back to work the next day, but I couldn't focus and had to go home. Maybe one of a total of half a dozen sick days in my 27-year career.

Biking was a great passion for me in Cuba. I had a fast bike that I bought in Miami. I wiped out once on an oil slick in the rain and still have a catch in my breastbone where I cracked it. But I managed to get into work that day and make it through the day, even though I looked like something the cat had dragged in. I'm a typical guy; I hate to go to the doc.

One of my biker friends was a former bike messenger and part of the new breed of Foreign Service officers. She was sharp, adventurous, committed, and attractive. She belied the old, sexist joke I heard from a Pentagon colleague – "What do you call a pretty girl at the State Department? A visitor." Sophia moved on to the NGO world, but she was a natural leader and would have been a great ambassador.

Another part of my job was prescreening refugee applicants. They consisted mostly of Jehovah's Witnesses who refused to serve in the military. One applicant was a beautiful young single Cuban mom. I took her information and passed it to the Immigration and Naturalization Service. Not long after I had a trip planned to Miami. A contact of the Interests Section contacted me and said the young woman had been granted refugee status and was in Miami. She wanted to thank me personally for my help and he gave me her address and telephone number. It seemed like a classic honey trap to me and I never called. Ops Sec – operational security – is kind of a 24/7 thing in the State Department.

I picked up hitchhikers often, just to pass the time and hear what they were thinking. One night I dropped off our maidservant and was turning around in her street when I was flagged down. It was late and I couldn't help but slow down to turn around. My hiker got in, started chatting and I immediately knew I had made a mistake; he was drunk. I could just make out that he was with the security services. He had a paper bag which I figured was a bottle of alcohol, but it turned out to be a gun. He waved it around, ranted some more, and finally I told him to get out. He did. I hit the gas and the door hit him on the head as I sped off.

We also heard shots one night at home. I went outside (dumb) and looked and there was a smiling plainclothes policeman taking a suspect away. Rule one when you hear shots; stay away from the window. Very hard to do.

The Websters were visiting from Finland. That night Anu put her Finnish passport under her pillow. You never know when real unrest could happen, but this was an isolated incident. For the most part Cuba was peaceful, and most people were fixated on just getting by during an extremely hard time economically.

Kathy also worked in the consular section. That was good as she was very good at finding opportunities. Spouses, or "eligible family members," are all talented and want to contribute. We've had spouses who were photographers, writers, nurses… I wish they could all be hired, especially at the small, hardship posts that are so understaffed like Havana.

The principal officer's residence was a sort of oasis. We celebrated the Fourth of July at the residence. A beautiful two-story house built with FDR (President Franklin Roosevelt) in mind as a place in which he could relax after the war. Although just two floors, with the classic diplomatic design of the entertaining or "representational" space downstairs, the really striking thing was the manicured gardens, palm trees, and swimming pool that the P.O. opened to the U.S. community on weekends. Independence Day was just hot dogs and coke, nothing fancy, but I remember seeing the American flag waving there and knowing that it was perhaps one of just two American flags flying in Cuba, the other being at the Interests Section on the Malecon. I was caught up short as we started the party with the pledge. The stark contrast of ideals, American and communist, were in sharp relief. I'd later get that same feeling driving down a Moscow street with the ambassador and the flags flying on the grill of the limo. Pretty special.

I did an environmental reporting cable in Cuba too. Much like reporting on events in the Baltics, our reports to Washington on Cuba gave policymakers a field perspective. Some of the best reporting I've ever seen came from the ambassadors in Russia, especially the "Scenesetter" cables that ambassadors write when an American president or SecState is visiting. The scene setter is meant to give the president an insight into the politics and the dynamics behind the scenes in the country he is planning to visit. Even in the midst of turmoil, the best scene setters beat the *New York Times* every time.

I reported on Cuba's environmental initiatives and had access to Cuban environment officials. Cuba had abandoned tractors for oxen and bicycles were big instead of cars, so there was plenty of good news, but Cuba had also planted tons of sugar cane and cut down old growth tropical forests in the process. I saw miles of crabs on a road near the Bay of Pigs. Just one car would have wiped out thousands of them. I never saw the famed ivory-billed woodpecker, but the lack of development and fast-food chains make Cuba a lovely looking destination. And there are some tiny museums that are gems, including one that claimed to have a wooden fragment of Christ's cross that was carried aboard Christopher Columbus' ship. For better or worse, Cuba is uniquely Cuba. As the song goes, "*Cuba, que linda es Cuba.*" (Cuba, how beautiful is Cuba.) Beautiful, frustrating, admirable, and alluring. You have to experience it to understand. The music, the antique cars that still cruise the streets, the beaches, and the countryside combine to make a culture as rich and smooth as a Cuban cigar.

STEP 10 – SWITCH CAREER TRACKS, GO TO THE NORTH POLE Washington, D.C. 1993–1995

The visa line had been grueling work but good. A consular tour should be part of every Foreign Service Officer orientation. You learn to make decisions, learn to say no, and learn about the host country from the people themselves. Still, I was looking forward to something new.

Q: So, what were you thinking about for your next tour?

ARMBRUSTER: The next tour I really wanted to go to was the Oceans, Environment and Science bureau and the job that interested me was Arctic Affairs Officer.

Q: It is just interesting that you go from arctic to tropical back to arctic.

ARMBRUSTER: You have picked up the pattern. Cold to hot stays pretty consistent.

The department decided to add a career track to the existing tracks of political, economic, consular, management and public diplomacy… namely, an Environment, Science, and technology track.

To get in I needed references and support from the Interests Section Principal Officer in Havana. He said he thought I needed "more seasoning." I'd had several run-ins with this P.O. First, I didn't send the plane from Miami with flood relief supplies until it was fully loaded. The P.O. had said that the plane could leave on Sunday, so I had lined up supplies to be delivered Saturday. He called Friday and wanted the plane to go immediately. I knew it would go half full, so I refused. I also reported the actual number of visa applications pending. We had always said that there was a backlog of 15,000 applications. I finally checked, counting them by hand, figuring that number had to go up or down over the weeks. It did. It went up to 30,000. That wasn't a happy staff meeting either. Finally, I remember being ordered to issue a visa, no questions asked. I couldn't promise that. That also steamed the boss. So I reached out to my old boss at the CBS station in Honolulu since he knew my work on science and the environment.

That seemed to do the trick. I bid on the polar affairs job and soon we were off to Washington for my first Washington assignment.

I might have smoked a Cuban cigar to celebrate, but they never did it for me. I also could have stashed a few boxes of Cuban cigars into my luggage – I think we were allowed two boxes per flight – but we never really got into them. The boxes are cool, and I like the smell of secondhand cigar smoke. It reminds me of my grandfather, but I was no connoisseur. Kathy toured the cigar factory and she enjoyed her stogie and looked good smoking it.

My boss told me on the first day that he was the most senior American official interested in polar affairs, so whatever we decided in polar affairs was likely to be U.S. policy.

We got straight to work on getting the Arctic Council up and running. To prove we could all cooperate in the region, the U.S. organized a mock nuclear accident. I coordinated the international participation. I traveled to Anchorage, Alaska for the RADEX 94 exercise. It was a "tabletop" simulation of a nuclear accident in "Arcticland," since it would have been impolitic to invite the Russians and role-play a meltdown at Bilibino Nuclear Power Plant, which was really what we were doing. Every country went through their evacuation protocols, iodine distribution, and alert communication networks and procedures. It was a good exercise, and a harbinger of the close cooperation to come through the Arctic Council. From lowly beginnings the Arctic Council event has now evolved into a ministerial or Secretary of State gathering, along with scientific, trade, and technical working groups and observers from all over the world.

On the margins of the conference my college friend Fred Smyth came to see me, and we rented kayaks on the Kenai Peninsula. We had a fantastic long race in the morning in which Fred took the direct route and I went out to sea, hoping the swells would propel me faster than the calm water near shore. Fred won. I had my usual camping food, sardines, including the juice. I drank some, stripped down and jumped in the cold Alaskan water for a swim. When I came back, Fred looked at me and said, "You're a hard man, Armbruster." We saw bald eagles and terrific scenery and thoroughly enjoyed ourselves on the water, even singing our college anthem *Saturday Night's Alright for Fighting* at the top of our lungs while paddling on the frigid water.

I also traveled to Norway for a conference where we went over a risk assessment matrix for the Arctic. Most of the risks came from Russia, from their nuclear contaminated rivers and sunken nuclear submarines. I said as much at the conference and again the Russians took it fairly well.

The best part of being a polar affairs officer was going to Greenland. Thule Air Base still serves as an important radar station and there are many American scientists who are in Greenland researching climate change. When I went to visit one of the science bases the pilot asked if I'd like to take part in Cool School. I said, "Sure."

The Greenland scientists are supported by the Schenectady, New York Airlift Wing and they run an exercise called "Cool School," a three-day Arctic survival course. I reported several months later to the base in New York, after getting no cost travel orders – which means that if I died I would be on duty and my family would be eligible for death benefits. We flew on a ski-equipped C-130, landed on the ice and the training began. The former Air Force instructor said, "You are never as good after an accident as when you first get out of the plane. In these conditions, you can only get weaker, so it's important to get your shelter set up, plus your signals to make yourself visible to search and rescue, and your food." We started digging.

The first night we made a snow shelter with a parachute over it and slept as one big group. The instructor said, "At this latitude there is no homophobia, everybody is 98 degrees so bunch up and stay warm." I couldn't even manage to keep my water bladder that we wore around our necks unfrozen. The second night we made our own two-man shelters. It was a lot of work, but I was too slow and the instructor showed me how it was done. We had a nice space, with the requisite step down where the really cold air went. It was close to minus 40 that morning – the same in Celsius and Fahrenheit at that temperature. We saw an

Arctic wolf, he followed us at a respectful distance hoping for scraps, not that military meals ready-to-eat are likely to have scraps.

And we saw the Danish ski patrols. Our instructors were all special forces types: quiet, reserved, and capable as hell. But the Danes were like Arctic gods. Completed unfazed by the temperature, happy on their skis, and the coolest guys on the planet as far as I was concerned. There wasn't much food to be had in the wild. Someone caught a shrew of some sort, but we didn't eat it. And there was no firewood either, so we lived off the supplies from the plane with double MRE (Meal Ready to Eat) rations. We made a latrine and marked where we were with parachutes and other colorful things, but our "town" didn't consist of much. A trick of light made it look like there was a real crystal city in the distance. Arctic mirages can be as real as desert mirages.

My polar coat had all the bells and whistles – shoulder lapels to pull someone out of an avalanche, an outside window for a watch, so you didn't have to expose your wrist, and a fur-lined hand warmer pocket, because inevitably you have to use your fingers for work requiring dexterity. It's great polar equipment. We finally got off the ice and went back to Thule. That hot shower was one of the greatest pleasures of my life.

State Magazine printed an article on "Cool School" in Greenland

Q: *Obviously the Arctic has lots of issues going on, certainly environmental issues, and issues of ownership and extractive drilling and all sorts of things that the public isn't aware of. So, at that time I guess it was now '93, what were the major issues going on for you in the Arctic?*

ARMBRUSTER: The Arctic Council was a nascent body, but they have taken on a lot of very substantive things: they have a working group on birds; they have something on persistent organic pollutants in the Arctic marine environment; and they have indigenous knowledge. They really take all of the Arctic countries and glean all the expertise that's possible, whether it's from scientists, politicians, or indigenous people so that there is some concerted effort to advance the lives of people there and that very important habitat. It was exciting to be in at the ground floor of the creation of the Arctic Council and I think it has become one of those bodies that works very well.

We also worked on Antarctic issues. Of course, the Antarctic has the Antarctic Treaty and all countries can do scientific work there. I think that is a model that would work in outer space and elsewhere, but there are fascinating issues and I have tried to stay current on polar issues. Now with global warming there are sea routes that didn't exist before and there is a lot of geopolitical rivalry with China and Russia staking their claims. As you said, huge resources, both extractive and animal resources and now the potential for tourism. So, to have an international body that can try to improve the way we develop in the Arctic is a good thing.

Q: *To what extent did NGOs play a role in the Arctic?*

ARMBRUSTER: At that point they were just beginning to have a role. They certainly observed meetings and other countries would as well. China was not formally in the Arctic Council but were also formally observing and participating because they saw it as an important international body. I don't think it would be fair to say they were shaping policy at that point. I think the NGOs are more powerful and now very much shape policy in the region.

Q: Was whaling an issue for you with the Arctic?

ARMBRUSTER: Yes. There are rights for some indigenous groups to take a certain number of whales. It was not very controversial because the take was fairly limited. We did not get into the Norwegian minke whale issue because that was handled by our delegates to the International Whaling Commission.

Q: I see. Yes, obviously because they are often migratory, so they are not necessarily always in the Arctic. What about fishing?

ARMBRUSTER: Fishing. Again the State Department has some real fishing experts who have been negotiating for years. There is something called the "donut hole." International treaties cover a large part of the ocean but then there is this hole that is not covered and that is where the fishing boats go. And of course, the fish transit and there is a big impact that we had hoped to avoid with these various treaties. So fishing is a big issue for the Arctic. I am sure it was near the top of the agenda in their latest meeting.

Q: OK, being in the department for the first time what were the other impressions or new learning you had. This is sort of the first time you are in the mother ship so to speak.

ARMBRUSTER: That is true and at that point I got the feeling that environmental issues were being taken very seriously. My follow-on assignment was George Washington's Elliott School for International Science and Technology Policy. I thought that was going to be the direction I was going to go in my career.

There was real resistance to providing any kind of environmental assistance to Russia. I wrote a paper on expanding U.S. environmental assistance to Russia that would go beyond our nuclear deals because of the public diplomacy payback we would get in return.

You know, you go to a Russian town and do something good for their environment and put the American seal on it, it is going to be good for us. The same as if you do schools or roads or hospitals. But the reaction in the department was definitely no.

Q: *But otherwise did you find it helpful to be in Washington for, let's say, planning your next assignment lobbying or finding a mentor who was going to give you a little bit of guidance about career planning, that sort of a thing?*

ARMBRUSTER: I have always known I am sort of a field guy. So, I knew that I didn't want to spend much time in Washington. I enjoyed working with the National Science Foundation and the opportunity that collaboration afforded me to get out of the building. I don't think being in the department was as formative for me as it might have been for others but I certainly worked with great people, like Ray Arnaudo, who was head of the Arctic Affairs unit and Tucker Scully who was in charge of oceans and was a real expert on the Antarctic Treaty. What I really learned from them was negotiations and just how to run a meeting with other countries. Occasionally I would be able to sit in the U.S. chair at an Arctic Council meeting. Usually It was Ray or Tucker or somebody else and to watch them at work was really enlightening for me.

Q: *There is negotiating at the table. There is also the kind of side bars, the informal activities. Did you do much of that? Did you find you were able to accomplish things outside of the negotiating room?*

ARMBRUSTER: Yes, and because the U.S. would field such a big delegation, a lot of times the negotiations that were the most intense were on our side of the table. For instance, the military were very cautious about what the U.S. was going to do and commit to in the Arctic, and they had real hard lines. So, we had to be careful about how far we could go and to what extent the U.S. could be involved in something. Yes, very much so. That inter-agency dynamic was something I was just beginning to learn, finding out that other agencies have real equity and you have to take them into account, because if you don't, your treaty, your agreement, is not going to hold up.

Q: So, you knew you were going to be doing work in the nuclear field; was it only civilian use or was it also being schooled a bit in nuclear weaponry?

ARMBRUSTER: The work that I was doing was a little bit of both. In Moscow the big agreement was what they called the HEU-LEU Agreement – highly enriched uranium to low enriched uranium which was a deal where the U.S. was buying HEU from the Russians, blending it down into low enriched uranium and burning it in civilian nuclear power plants so it really was a swords-to-plowshares arrangement. The Russians made a lot of money from it. Unfortunately, it was not the kind of an opportunity where the average Russian saw much of a result. So again, we lost that opportunity to build a school so that the average Russian could say, "Oh the Americans built that school," or "My kid was born in the American hospital." I think we missed the Marshall Plan[5] opportunity with the Russians, but the nuclear deal was important. We worked with the Ministry of Atomic Energy on that. There was a program called the Nuclear Cities Initiative[6] going to formerly closed cities like Sarov – previously called Arzamas-16 – and trying to develop civilian professions and careers for those nuclear scientists so they didn't sell their service to Iran or North Korea. There were programs to upgrade fences, cameras, and accounting of nuclear materials. You know, it was really a full court press often led by the Department of Energy,

---

5   Officially the European Recovery Program (ERP), the Marshall Plan was an American initiative passed in 1948 to aid Western Europe, in which the United States gave over $12 billion in economic assistance to help rebuild Western European economies after the end of World War II.

6   A nonproliferation program within the National Nuclear Security Administration of the U.S. Department of Energy. The purpose of NCI was to enhance U.S. and global security by supporting weapons complex reduction in Russian nuclear cities. The NCI worked in cooperation with MinAtom (Ministry for Atomic Energy of the Russian Federation) to redirect functions and equipment in the weapons complex; reduce the physical footprint; and create sustainable, alternative nonweapons work within a functioning city economy. https://www.nap.edu/read/10392/chapter/2

but State had a coordinating role. I would often be control officer for Senator Domenici who had a real interest in these issues or for the visiting Department of Energy (DOE) official, often Rose Gottemoeller, who became Under Secretary of State for Arms Control and International Security. So, it was a pretty hopeful time for cooperation. The Russians still resented the fact that we won the Cold War if you want to put it that way. One official from the Ministry of Atomic Energy said to me, "You destroyed us." When I visited Arzamas-16 with Senator Domenici the ballrooms there, the grand pianos and everything was dilapidated, and I realized that when the Cold War ended we had indeed destroyed the way of life for the elite Soviet nuclear scientist or policymaker.

Polar Affairs was my only full Washington assignment during my 28-year career. I did spend time in the U.S. in language school, at the Naval War College, and at George Washington University, and heck, Nuevo Laredo, Mexico was a bike ride away from Laredo, Texas, but if you want to do well, conventional wisdom says spend some time in Washington, preferably on the 7th floor where the secretary and assistant secretaries live. At a class reunion my A-100 classmates voted me least likely to be spotted in Washington. I was told about that later as I didn't actually make the reunion. So, do your time in D.C. Ideally, every third tour or so. Makes your mom happy too.

STEP 11 – GET SMARTER
Washington, D.C. 1995–1997

Aside from language training, there are other opportunities for education. Take 'em! I took advantage of every training opportunity I could get.

Q: So how was Russian training for you?

ARMBRUSTER: I liked it a lot. I am one of those learners that likes all sorts of media. I like to watch the movies; I like to look at the newspaper; I like dialog. I like it to come at me with a fire hose. I think I got either a 3 or a 3+ in Russian from that. I later got a 4/4 the second time to Russia, but I just found the native-speaking Russian teachers at FSI to be excellent. They really knew how to make you work to understand the grammar and put it into operation. I learned more about English grammar than I ever did before with the instrumental case and accusative and subjunctive and all that stuff. I enjoyed it a lot. I mean to be paid to learn languages is really a privilege.

From polar affairs I went to George Washington University's Elliott School of International Affairs. That one-year program was to prepare me as the environment officer in Embassy Moscow. That really sounded terrific. I met the science counselor before going to post and he said, "No, you're going to be Nuclear Affairs Officer. That's where I need you." I thought about it a bit, knew it was something of a bait and switch, but decided that nuclear affairs really is one of the biggest environmental issues. The lesson too is to always take the position with the most responsibility. While the environment portfolio would have been interesting, the nuclear job was heftier and turned out to be fascinating.

Allan Flanigan, who had been my principal officer in Havana, invited me to his swearing-in ceremony as ambassador to El Salvador. He said it was always his dream to be ambassador "to a country that mattered." We shook hands after the ceremony, and he asked where

I was off to. I said, "Nuclear Affairs in Moscow." He said, "That's a real job."

It was good to take a break and immerse myself in the complexity of nuclear issues and U.S. space policy. One highlight was our class meeting with the head of NASA for an informal meeting. We asked about safety, given the space shuttle *Challenger* disaster. The administrator made it clear that some national security goals require sacrifices. Safety is always a priority, but astronauts know they are signing up for hazardous duty, no less than soldiers and they'll do their duty and take risks to further a noble cause. Space exploration is one of those causes. I agree with him, and think we are often too quick to set limits on diplomats serving abroad. We are too quick to bring them home, and too quick to restrict them to the compound. We know the risks and are happy to take them. In fact, sometimes we are safer by getting out in public, learning from local people, and showing we are not two-headed monsters after all. In embassies, we build security with walls, guards, and metal detectors. Contrast that with the Peace Corps who build security with relationships, living in the community, and trust. In both cases we take risks for a larger cause. It's not the same service as the military and I would never equate the risks, but there are plaques honoring Peace Corps volunteers, foreign service officers, and NASA astronauts and I'll bet every family would tell you that not one of the fallen would have traded their experience for the world.

I took a crash course in nukes from the Department of Energy, got my Q clearance, DOE's special clearance for nuclear issues, and got ready for the tour.

Before heading to Moscow I had some time to take a negotiations course taught by the *Getting to Yes* authors.[7] I learned that while "the lion gets the lion's share" in a negotiation, it really helps to go beyond positions and try to understand the underlying motivation of the other side. The other key takeaway was that

---

[7] https://play.google.com/store/books/details/Roger_Fisher_Getting_to_Yes?id=SgONZTjbqpgC

negotiating with those on your side of the table is as important as negotiating with those on the other side.

I also spent some time at the Russia Desk in Washington where I was assigned to be a lead negotiator for an agreement with Russia on emergency response. The Federal Emergency Management Agency (FEMA) was the lead agency on the U.S. side with the Russian equivalent, EMERCOM,[8] on the other side. The impetus for the agreement was the *Exxon Valdez* spill.[9] The Russians offered the U.S. an oil skimmer that they had in the Arctic to help with the initial clean up. U.S. lawyers decided that with no liability agreement in place it was a no-go. At that time, U.S.-Russian cooperation was high and the aim was to have this agreement negotiated in time for the next Gore-Chernomyrdin meeting in Moscow. Vice President Gore was going to lead the delegation and I was sent to Moscow several weeks ahead of time to see if I could broker an agreement. FEMA gave me enough leeway to be flexible and it looked like we could do it. I think we finished with an agreed upon text about 11 p.m. the night before the signing ceremony.

Russian skimmer

8   The Ministry of Emergency Situations, MChS, or known internationally as EMERCOM (derived from Emergency Control Ministry).

9   https://www.eenews.net/stories/1060128041; https://mashable.com/2014/03/24/exxon-valdez-25-years-later/

That evening at a reception in Spaso House, Al Gore made his way over to me. I was all set to tell him about how this would be a great thing for the Arctic and the environment in general. One of his embassy handlers adroitly moved Gore on to bigger fish though, so I didn't have a chance for a one-on-one with the man himself.

I should have worked out a more elegant title for the agreement. Even in English, it sounds Russian:

> MEMORANDUM OF UNDERSTANDING BETWEEN THE GOVERNMENT OF THE RUSSIAN FEDERATION AND THE GOVERNMENT OF THE UNITED STATES OF AMERICA ON COOPERATION IN NATURAL AND MAN-MADE TECHNOLOGICAL EMERGENCY PREVENTION AND RESPONSE.

Signed Moscow, 16 JUL 1996.

The rest of it read like Shakespeare, trust me.

STEP 12 – BACK TO MOSCOW
Moscow, Russia 1997–2000

I arrived in Moscow for my full assignment on a morning flight, was picked up by the Environment, Science and Technology Minister Counselor and was taken to work for a full day. It didn't take long to see that the nuclear portfolio was a big job and I made sure I was up and running in no time. For Kathy and the kids it was a good tour too.

Q: *How did the family feel about going to Russia?*

ARMBRUSTER: Kalia was probably a little bit too young to resist, but our son was right at that high school age where resistance was absolutely what he wanted to do. For the first week or something he was miserable. 'I hate this. I want to go back.' Then he started to realize 'I can ride the metro. I can go into a bar with my friends. I can travel to Belgium with the soccer team and play soccer for my school!' It didn't take him long to realize that this was the best gig any high school kid could have. He even got scuba certified in the Red Sea on vacation. Kalia got involved in theater and is now really into Improv in San Francisco. It was a formative tour. So with Kathy working at the Anglo-American school where I had worked years before, albeit a different location in town, for us as a family in a lot of ways Moscow was our best post. We were all there together. Everybody was engaged in things and we liked it quite a lot.

Q: *What was the embassy like when you arrived in 97?*

ARMBRUSTER: Jim Collins was the ambassador. As always it is a very high tempo embassy. I think morale for the most part was pretty good, but I think morale is always better among people who speak the language better – that is true for spouses as well. The single biggest determinant of morale and effectiveness is language ability, but as far as the construction and the move I didn't find that to be disruptive. We still did our work; we could walk to the foreign ministry and have meetings there. There were frequently many high-level visitors. I was control officer for President Clinton. I think the embassy thrived on that kind of thing. And the countdown meetings, where we walked through every step of the visit, was a chance for everyone to contribute. It was an embassy where people worked hard and probably didn't get a lot of recognition. Like the ambassador once said, "You people don't get a lot of thanks for all that you do but, thank you, it is important work." I think people found an intrinsic reward in being in Moscow at that time and working on the issues that we worked on.

With the Soviet Union now history I had an opportunity to test just how open the new Russia would be. We had detected a "seismic event" in the Kola peninsula, not far from a military base, and the obvious question was whether the earthshaking event was some sort of subcritical nuclear test. I had some contacts, thanks to the year at GW University, so I set up a meeting and asked the Russian scientist about it. He said he would meet back with me in a couple of days. We met again and I could tell I was treading on difficult ground, but I pressed anyway, asking as many questions as I could. The next day, on the bus back to our residential compound, I opened my newspaper only to see a red laser dot dancing on the page. Message received. I was angry, especially that a threat would be made on a shuttle bus with other people, including school-children, on it.

That didn't stop me from doing a lot of work on nuclear issues. I traveled to nuclear power plants all over Russia, as well as Sarov – or Arzamas-16 – the laboratory at the heart of the Soviet nuclear program. I arranged for Senator Pete Domenici to go to Sarov too to see about U.S. cooperation on the Nuclear Cities program, a program to bring Russia's top-secret scientists back into the fold and keep them from selling their secrets.

We rented a small plane and made the trip to the city that was also a religious mecca before the Cold War due to a sacred spring and a Russian saint[10] but had become a Soviet nuclear fortress. Where the U.S. put fences around labs in Los Alamos and elsewhere, the Soviets put fences around whole cities. Those cities became privileged enclaves with the best schools, restaurants, and infrastructure.

Domenici had a meeting with one of Russia's admirals. The U.S. was concerned about the safety of nuclear subs. I was the notetaker. Domenici went at the admiral hard, saying, "You've got problems with your fleet in the Arctic. You've got problems in the Pacific…"

The Admiral cut him off. "We don't have problems," he said, "We have tasks." That was one of the best quotes I'd heard expressing the Russian military mentality. Undoubtedly part of the ethos that helped the Soviets beat the Nazis in WWII. They took tremendous losses but kept on.

Domenici took a real interest in Russia and visited several times. I was going to be John Kerry's control officer too for an extensive trip throughout Russia. Unfortunately, the Kosovo bombing campaign derailed the trip. That was the beginning of the distrust that torpedoed U.S.-Russian cooperation. Not that the bombing campaign was a mistake, but maybe more diplomacy would have been in order with Russia before punishing their Serbian allies. Russia always thought, 'If the U.S. can bomb the Serbs for bad behavior, they can bomb us.'

While I was still at George Washington University, I told one of their science professors about the posting. He asked what I thought about it. This was after Chernobyl and I said, "Well, anything I can do to discourage nuclear energy would be a good thing." He said, "Well, you won't be a very good representative for America then." He believed in nuclear power. The longer I was in Moscow, and the more I met with scientists from both sides, the more I came to realize that future generations of nuclear power could be safe: graphite reactors, smaller reactors, reactors that burned excess plutonium. There was still something to be

---

[10]   In the earlier history of Russia it was known as one of the holy places of the Russian Orthodox Church, because of its monastery that gave Russia one of its greatest saints, St Seraphim. Since the 1940s, it has gradually become the center for research and production of Soviet and later Russian nuclear weapons. https://en.wikipedia.org/wiki/Sarov

said for nuclear energy and if they could work together American and Russian scientists could come up with the next generation of clean energy.

Nuclear weapons are another story. Stewardship lasts for thousands of years. They cost a fortune, and the payoff is minimal. The U.S. maybe needs twelve. Using a nuclear weapon is so indiscriminate it can only be considered a crime against humanity. In short, it's time for almost all swords to be turned to plowshares, or something like that...

Some of our most important work at the embassy at the time was doing just that, for example, the U.S.-Russian HEU-LEU agreement, which ran until December 2013, was good for security and provided Russia with badly needed cash. My job at the embassy was attending the meetings of the negotiators to keep the agreement on track. The American side was not always sure the fissile material was coming from missiles and was of the high grade that was advertised. And the Russians distrusted the American side. So the negotiations were fun to report and send back to Washington.

Q: *Now who were your principal interlocutors on the Russian side?*

ARMBRUSTER: For us it was the Ministry of Atomic Energy - Minister Adamov. A pretty taciturn guy who could be difficult. We would have the Secretary of Energy come out often for high-level talks. There was also the Gore-Chernomyrdin process at that point so there were a lot of multilateral initiatives going on in different areas. The exciting thing about the relationship then - as opposed to the Cold War - was that during the Cold War it was all about the security relationship, but as things thawed, we could talk about issues to do with civilian travel, tourism, education, cultural differences, the environment, etc. The whole spectrum was on the table for the Gore-Chernomyrdin meetings.

Q: *What were your goals or what goals were you given during your tour there in the nuclear field?*

ARMBRUSTER: I was meeting with the Russians every day, reporting on what the Russians would and wouldn't allow in terms of cooperation. I worked a lot with the inter-agency community on getting the intelligence and the reporting we needed to sort of figure out just how far we could push the Russians. So, for example, the Nuclear Cities Initiative ended up not being feasible. The funds for that were basically turned off mainly because the Russians said, "No, we are not going to give you access to those scientists or those cities the way you want." I think what we were seeing was a slow retreat by the Russians from full cooperation with the United States on nuclear issues. But had we really pursued it we could have had more work on a program called Plutonium Management and Disposition Agreement,[11] for example. What do we do with these tons of plutonium that both countries have to dispose? Can we work together and put our scientists together to figure out ways to safely dispose of it? Also, we were working on some of the advanced nuclear reactors. Could our scientists cooperate in those areas? So, those are still things that we could theoretically do together. But it just seemed like the Russian motto was "we are not going to just roll over and take your money." We had a lot of ideas and we had a lot of programs that were ready to go. The Russians just couldn't bear the thought of working that closely with us, I think, that soon after the Cold War.

Q: That was sort of on the Russian side. Did the Russians have any interest in anything we were doing, the U.S. in domestic civilian nuclear energy?

ARMBRUSTER: I think they were interested in the advanced reactors.

Q: Take a second to explain what an advanced reactor would be.

ARMBRUSTER: Next generation fusion reactors that would produce enormous amounts of power. The Russians were also working on sort of the opposite end of the spectrum, graphite reactors and safer reactors that used lower levels of uranium or plutonium or

---

11   http://fissilematerials.org/library/PMDA2010.pdf

whatever the fuel was. Such that even if a plane crashed into the plant there would not be a catastrophic release of radioactivity. So, there were some pretty promising avenues. If we were going to develop nuclear technology the Americans and the Russians were two of the key players in the world, along with the French and the Japanese. Really the Russians were pretty advanced. I wasn't involved in the START agreement (Strategic Arms Reduction Treaty) or the military side because we had military folks dealing directly with their military installations and doing the same thing that the Department of Energy was doing on the civilian side. I toured a bunch of nuclear reactors and got to see the glowing rods inside. It was a little scary.

I was control officer for the NRC director who came over to St Petersburg and Moscow. She was working with the Russians on that. How can you safely extend the life of a nuclear plant? So, there were a lot of issues. I was there for three years. The third year I actually went from the Environment, Science and Technology (EST) section to the political section as Baltic Affairs officer. So, I was working on trade issues and, as you said, broad issues across the board, not just nuclear.

Q: In your work with your issues on the Baltics you focused principally on trade you say?

ARMBRUSTER: It was trade and Russian Baltic relations. The Russian diaspora in the Baltics and how that affected politics. There were some minor U.S. initiatives for regional development, something called the Northeast Europe Initiative, but it never had much money. And so, it was really more the normal diplomacy of meeting with the Baltic diplomats and comparing notes on how they saw Russia's development. But it was clear that the Baltics were taking a different path from Russia.

Q: OK, there was only one nuclear reactor, but were they themselves interested in getting a nuclear reactor as an alternative source?

ARMBRUSTER: No, I don't think so. When I think of the Baltic countries, I think of them as being sort of more progressive on the leading edge on the environment, looking at clean technologies and being much more at home and natural partners with the other Nordic countries. In fact, each of those countries sort of adopted a Baltic country. I think Norway was Latvia and Finland was Estonia and so on, but I was impressed with the Baltic leaders. They were young and idealistic and some American – some people with Baltic heritage who had become Americans – had come back and taken leadership roles. As a region it is a success story.

Q: *This was the very early days of the idea of expanding NATO. Did that play when you were there?*

ARMBRUSTER: It did, and it was controversial, and of course the Russians had a knee-jerk reaction to it, because they perceived it as a threat. Some people second-guessed whether it rolled out the correct way but the whole idea of international relations is that each country is allowed to make their own choices about their friends and allies, so I am glad they are in NATO. They are good partners. They have had to put up with a lot of Russian shenanigans. I think the Russians will continue to be troublesome in those areas. The thing about borders is when you see a vibrant busy border crossing you know things are healthy and going right. But at that point, even then trade between Russia and some of the Baltic countries was really limited, and you'd go to these border crossings and you knew almost nothing was happening there. They should have been vibrant crossing points and a mixing of people and commerce and culture.

Q: *Was that a mutual choice or did you get the impression that the Baltics were really trying to reorient everything West.*

ARMBRUSTER: I think that was more driven by the Russians. I think they wanted to punish the Baltics for leaning toward the West. You are right. I think that some in the Baltics would be just as happy to turn their backs on Russia and not look back, but I think now there is a more pragmatic view that if they could get along with Russia and trade with them it is a win for both sides.

Q: *Were you expecting to do a bit of work on space in Moscow?*

ARMBRUSTER: Space is a really rich area of cooperation. That is one thing that has survived throughout all these years. All of our astronauts get to space thanks to a Russian spacecraft. Other than meeting with the NASA people in the embassy, later in Vladivostok we hosted an astronaut for a public diplomacy event, and I got to see a cosmonaut and an astronaut interact again. Astronauts and cosmonauts are bigger than rock stars; everybody loves them!

———◆———

I was also control officer for President Clinton's trip. Chances are I volunteered. I recall one of my bosses saying, "Armbruster, you always volunteer. Why?" Of course it was more hours, with days lasting from early morning until midnight, but it was always fun. And motor pool usually took me home in a rented Mercedes when I was done for the day. (I remember as Sonny Bono's control officer I thought I was doing pretty well, getting him back to his hotel by midnight, only to see his picture in the paper the next day at a classy nightclub that he went to after I dropped him off.)

President Clinton's trips had several "off the record" events. That was my responsibility. One was to go to a church, another a drop by at a bakery.

The big row between the U.S. and the Russian protective details had the Russians pushing for more public access. The U.S. Secret Service wanted a cordon backed up to the corner where pedestrians would not be allowed. The FSB[12] said, "Look, this is a big deal for our people, they want to see the president. It doesn't seem very democratic not to let them have a look at him.' I was translating all of this

---

[12]   Federalnaya Sluzhba Bezopasnosti, formerly (1994–95) Federal Counterintelligence Service, Russian internal security and counterintelligence service created in 1994 as one of the successor agencies of the Soviet-era KGB.

back and forth. Finally, one of the Russians said, "Hey, I have to tell you this, the crowd that will be across the street… half of them will be our guys anyway," and he patted his coat pocket to indicate they would be armed. The lead Secret Service agent thought about it a minute and said, "Yeah. That is the Russian way. OK." And the Pushkin Cafe visit was on.

I went upstairs at one point to check on the president and his party. It was off the record, so I won't say who he was with, but he looked happy, smoking a cigar. As I drew closer, he saw me, smiled and looked approachable enough, but I headed back downstairs, figuring I had done my job getting him there and he was happy.

The advance team had worked out which shop he would visit; I think it was a butcher shop and they had switched the shopkeeper with a pretty girl from the bakery next door. The Secret Service radio crackled, "We're five minutes out." Everybody shifted, and smiled, ready for the visit. "Four minutes." I made my way to the door, to make sure it was open for his party. "Pushkin team, we're diverting to the Christ the Savior church. Church team standby." I'm not sure if they diverted for security reasons, or if they simply asked the Clintons if they wanted to go to the church or the Russian shop? I'll never know.

I was also control officer for a rising Republican political star, Condoleezza Rice. She was coming to Moscow to debate with her Democratic counterpart Chip Blacker. When she arrived at Sheremetyevo Airport, we went to a VIP holding room to wait for her luggage. With big VIPs we have a separate driver for the luggage and a General Services Officer (GSO) waits for it while the VIP goes directly to the hotel. But the embassy just sent me, no luggage van, so we waited for her bags. We chatted and I found her very engaging, despite the long flight.

At the meetings in Moscow Condi Rice was relaxed, confident, and on point. Chip Blacker never seemed to quite catch up from jet lag. If we were scoring the debate the future Secretary of State would have won hands down. And I'm not a Republican.

One of Condoleezza's reforms as Secretary of State was to "rebalance" our presence overseas. The State Department had embraced the idea of "universality" that the U.S. is important enough to be everywhere. Secretary Rice wisely moved employees from European posts like Hamburg to new missions in Central Asia and India. That's smart. And we do need diplomats everywhere. If you can find an American pastor in need of help in Sakhalin, Russia, and hikers in the wilds of the Pamir mountains in Central Asia, you can be sure you will still need real, live breathing diplomats, and not just a "virtual presence." The idea that you can serve Americans abroad and American interests with video calls and chat rooms is an idea I disdain. A virtual post is no post at all.

But, back to Moscow. The nuclear work continued and my respect for my Russian colleague only increased. Every embassy relies on Foreign Service Nationals, people that we hire from the host country. We used to hire in the top 80 percent of local salaries, taking the very best talent, although probably not getting the folks who went to IBM or Boeing or any of the other top tier international companies. My FSN (Foreign Service National), Alexei Davidov, was a veteran, not of the war, but of Chernobyl. When the disaster happened, he worked for the Russian equivalent of the Nuclear Regulatory Commission. Luckily, he was at his dacha when the units went critical and it took his office a day or two to track him down in the countryside. That saved his life, since the first responders arrived without safety gear. Alexei was given some crude safety protection, but he was exposed. He now has a lifelong pass on the Moscow Metro as a hero of Russia. Had he not been at his dacha, his death mask would have been with the others in Mitino, outside Moscow.

I visited Mitino on one of the Chernobyl anniversaries. People left bottles of vodka and bread by the markers of the young men who died in the initial days of the disaster. A young girl placed flowers by the mask of one of her relatives and smoothed her hand along his face. It was hard not to be moved. Like most FSN's, Alexei was dedicated to his country, but knew that improved relations with the U.S. would be a win-win. I also admired the embassy's DOE staff, local and American, and knew that they were advancing U.S. interests throughout Russia by making weapons facilities safer. Unfortunately, the cooperation, much of it under the Nunn-Lugar program,[13] was gradually pulled back by the Russians. I often said they were not going to just roll over and take our money. Maybe the Russians themselves would never have allowed a Marshall Plan.

Along with traveling to nuclear plants I had an opportunity to travel to Magadan, once the end of the line for Gulag prisoners. There is a Gulag museum there, with whole novels written on string, with each knot representing a word. Prisoners were inventive but working in the gold mine was deadly all the same. There is also a monument to the victims of the Gulag on the outskirts of town, *Mask of Sorrow*, a huge concrete mask with tears in the form of human beings, conveying some of the pain inflicted on Russia by Stalin.

Mask of Sorrow, The New Yorker. https://www.newyorker.com/culture/photo-booth/searching-for-memory-of-the-gulags-in-putins-russia

But our mission was not cultural or historical. I was sent with John Laahs, an Air Force officer, to coordinate a humanitarian relief flight from Anchorage. Magadan was experiencing a longer and colder than usual winter. The relief flight from the City of Anchorage had the basics – rice, cooking oil, sanitary supplies, just the essentials. It was cold and the Sea of Okhotsk had frozen. Even a wave breaking on the shore was frozen in time. We got to work, calling Moscow, Washington, and Anchorage at various points in the day to get all the clearances. My Russian was good – good enough to negotiate a treaty in Russian, but John's was better, at least on logistics.

---

[13]   The Department of Defense Cooperative Threat Reduction (CTR) Program, also known as the Nunn-Lugar Program, was created for the purpose of securing and dismantling weapons of mass destruction and their associated infrastructure in the former states of the Soviet Union. https://armscontrolcenter.org/fact-sheet-the-nunn-lugar-cooperative-threat-reduction-program/

We really put our diplomacy to use on the ice. The big Russian boss sent us out with his buddies to go king crab fishing before the C-130 arrived with the supplies. We were catching crabs, but I couldn't tell if the point was to catch crabs through the ice hole or to toast to everything under the sun with vodka. I do not compete with Russians in drinking, chess, or ice hockey. I had to do something. It was sunny, around minus 10, so not crazy cold, so I took my clothes off and did a polar bear (*Morzh*) plunge through the ice hole.

"King crabs" - a fitting moniker

I froze and tried to warm up afterward in the jeep. Actually at that point the vodka tasted damn good and there was no way it was going to get me drunk, just warm! I had proved my manhood, I was now one of the guys and we were friends for life, – or at least the duration of the mission. When the boss, and I never figured out if he was the governor or the local mafia heavy, heard about my swim he asked his guys, "Did you guys jump in?" "No, they said," He shot back, "You're fired!"

John and I could only find carbonated water, so we boiled that in the hotel for tea. I left a tip every morning for the maid, but every evening when I came home although the room was beautifully outfitted the money was never touched.

When the C-130 touched down the Russian troops were not happy. To them, it was shameful to get help from anyone, let alone the Americans. It was a windy and cold day and the transfer went fine.

I did some interviews at a local TV station. I knew the relief flight was a sensitive subject and I asked our young Russian minder if what I said was ok. He looked at me and said, "You said what you said, don't worry about it!" From then I said that to myself after every interview.

John and I both wrote up our reports. Mine emphasized the young people I met, the economic prospects, and the university. John had a look into the criminal activities, thanks to his excellent Russian and capacity to hold his vodka. Later, I heard it said in Washington, "So which city is it, the good one Armbruster wrote about, or the bad one Laahs described?" It was both and still is.

———————— ◆ ————————

The Russian circus is a joy. I'm sure the Humane Society would disagree, but I often saw I bond between trainer and lion or dog or monkey…. or cat. I've learned a few things about the Russian circus. One, a clown cannot pick up three things at once. One thing will fall. It's a law. And two, when it is time for audience participation, they *always* pick the bald guy. Yes, I was in the cat circus. The cats can walk on wires and do all sorts of tricks, but they can also do handstands balancing on the bald guy's hands. One cat in each hand. Meanwhile, the evil cat conductor threw plastic rings that landed perfectly over the bald guy's head, settling in a nice plastic necklace. The cats were unfazed and remained standing on their front paws on the bald guy's hands. It was utterly humiliating. But I loved it.

I'm not a fan of zoos for the most part and find the animals there are crazy bored, but the circus animals know they are stars. My wife will tell you I also have a thing for the Russian hoop girls. They really keep those hula hoops in motion!

We saw the Old Circus and the New Circus in Moscow as well as the circus in Minsk and Vladivostok. If diplomacy didn't work out, I figured I had a second calling as one of the clowns.

My last year in Moscow, 1999–2000 I transferred out of the science section and into the political section. While still doing nuclear stuff I saw an ad in *Scientific American* looking for a South Pole station manager. I applied. The interview was good, and I had my head around a year away from my family, but the logistics of getting them home, getting Bryan through his senior year of high school, and figuring out my onward assignment seemed insurmountable. It was a good opportunity, particularly for an environment, science and tech officer, but I took myself out of the running. Both kids liked Moscow and they both took the metro on their own. The Anglo-American school, where I once taught gym, now had kids regularly flying to Brussels for sports matches, or Norway for drama programs. It had grown.

I did not like the political job. While nuclear cooperation was well funded and the DOE had imaginative programs like the Nuclear Cities Initiative, there was little money for political initiatives. In the nuclear section we the HEU program mentioned earlier; we had programs to safeguard their weapons facilities with new cameras, sensors, and alarms, and we were trying to find a way to dispose of plutonium. But on the political side we were doing little to advance Russian democracy and civil society and Russians were hurting. Living off the food they could grow at their dachas, selling their clothes on the street, prostitution. It was desperate and international assistance was needed. We did bail them out with some structural loans but in the end the ruble crashed and the country seemed about to fall apart. They needed a Marshall Plan. And it never came. In part because they still had nuclear weapons, but we should have placed a bigger bet on their future.

There were some real joys living in Moscow. The Bolshoi, Red Square, Pushkin Cafe, even McDonald's was an adventure. And then there were the getaways to Helsinki and, even better, the ski week vacations we took in Portugal and the Canary Islands. I got my scuba certification in the Canaries and we always arrived in time for their big Mardi Gras type festival.

In Moscow we lived in Rosinka, an expat community northwest of Moscow, a long way from downtown. The Russian Olympic cross-country team practiced in the forest there and I often took people from the embassy on the trails. There were great up and downhill runs to the course, and you could really get going downhill. If it was minus 15 or above, our dog Chessie would come along. At below minus 15 she just did her business and went straight back into the house. One of the maintenance guys knew I loved skiing and he took me to his apartment way out of town. We skied on the frozen Volga river there. Another great memory.

I've always thought Moscow would lend itself well to having a commercial building right next to the embassy. Something like a "Main Street USA." In the old days American Express was a meeting place abroad. Americans would welcome a place to gather, get on Wi-Fi, have cultural events, etc. Why not open it up to American eateries and movie theaters? I know security is an issue, but I still think it could work in a lot of major cities with embassies or consulates.

One of my regular skiers was the Consul General. She was ready to take on the Olympic training trails in the forest and enjoyed the respite from her busy job providing visas and helping Americans in trouble. One day she asked if I would be interested in a job in a consulate as the principal officer. I would be the lead U.S. representative in a consular district. She was pitching Nuevo Laredo, Mexico, right across from Laredo, Texas. I'd be taking orders from the ambassador in Mexico City. He would visit the border once a year or so, and I'd get back to the embassy to kiss the ring once a year too. It was an opportunity for a leadership job. I hadn't gotten my first choice, to work on Russian issues at the National Security Council, so… "*Davai!*" as the Russians say, "Let's go!" Or to use Yuri Gagarin's phrase when he was the first man blasted into space, "*Poexali!* We're out of here!"

STEP 13 – PUTTING ON A SHERIFF'S BADGE ON THE BORDER
Nuevo Laredo, México 2000–2003

This was a start down a different path. A leadership path. The department had done away with the Environment Science and Technology track. I was now a Political Officer. I heard later that the Under Secretary for Global Affairs wasn't impressed with the EST officers – too nerdy – he preferred the high-flying political officers, often considered – especially by themselves – the cream of the crop. Most of the science officers became econ officers, but I never knew much about economics, so I embarked on my third career track.

My first interview with the Mexican media took place in the consul general's backyard.

The first question, "What is your first priority, Mr. Consul General?"

I said, "I believe drug trafficking is the gravest challenge facing us on the border, but the U.S. and Mexico can work together as we have done over the years to solve the problem. Drug trafficking erodes institutions, is harmful to our kids, and leads to violence."

The journalist paused, was about to say something, then went on to other questions. The next day in the news, the article about the new consul said, "Consul Armbruster's first priority is to promote tourism." He was trying to give me a chance not to get killed my first week on the job. I hope his instincts protected him. Many Nuevo Laredo journalists were killed, even if they wrote innocuous stories, simply because they were journalists and knew too much.

Most of our challenges in the consulate stemmed from drug violence or Americans in prison. My introduction wasn't an easy one. Arturo, the Foreign Service National, was at my elbow and seemed nervous. "What's up?" I asked.

"There's an American in the prison and he's not fitting in."

"What do you mean, he's not fitting in?" I asked.

"He's just not fitting in."

"Well, it's not a social club. He doesn't have to be popular."

"I know, but it makes me nervous."

Maybe I could get out to the prison in the next couple of days. The prisoner had been visited twice, but it sounded like I should go. We were the third busiest visa post in the world, so we had plenty of issues and plenty of work, but protection of American citizens is always at the top of the agenda. I often visited the 30 odd Americans we had in prisons up and down the border in our jurisdiction stretching from Nuevo Laredo, to Piedras Negras, to Ciudad Acuña. In this instance I filed the information away and did not set a date to go. My advice to you: when one of the locals is nervous, you should get nervous.

Two days later we got word that the American in question was dead. Beaten to death by fellow inmates, apparently because he was raving and urinated on his cellmates. He was in withdrawal from drug addiction and not coping well. The American was buried in a pauper's grave when we failed to find American next of kin. Six weeks later, my deputy, Lana Chumley, received a call asking if we'd had any contact with a man named Willis. She said, "No, but we had a recent prisoner by another name." It didn't take Lana long to connect the dots; Willis had provided a false name upon arrest and imprisonment.

I contacted the Mexican authorities and we met at the pauper's grave. They exhumed the body, by then a skeleton and I can still see one of the diggers holding up his skull like someone in a Shakespeare play. We got the remains transported over the border to the U.S. side. I met with the mother and tried to sympathetically weather her venting of grief, frustration, and anger.

The lessons for me were to follow up on any lead, no matter how seemingly trivial, like "someone not fitting in" and to always seek a Privacy Act Waiver from Americans in trouble. Privacy Act Waivers allow us to get in touch with the families. In some cases, the families don't want anything to do with the individual, but more often they come through with money or help. I don't know how we could have gotten his real name, since prisoners don't always have ID on them, we just accept what they write on the form but try to establish the identity and get the waiver.

The New York Times reported:

> *During the night of Sept. 17, Mr. Abell became agitated and wandered around the cell where he was being held with 60 other inmates, according to Mexican officials. Mumbling incoherently, the officials said, he stumbled repeatedly over prisoners who were trying to sleep.*
>
> *At least four prisoners and one guard severely beat Mr. Abell, who then lay unconscious until he was taken to a hospital on Sept. 21, where he was pronounced dead.*
>
> *Mexican officials have pledged to prosecute those responsible. And as a corrective measure, the Mexican government has now agreed that Americans at La Loma will be housed together, which the inmates believe will improve their safety, Tom Armbruster, an official with the United States consulate here, said today.*
>
> *It took six weeks for Mrs. Blount, 68, of San Antonio, to be notified by consular officials of her son's arrest, and by then he was already dead.*
>
> *"If they had just told me he was there," she said, "I would have gotten him out that very day, and he would still be alive."*

That was not our only case of unknown identity. I was lucky to have a retired officer working on American citizen issues. Dick McCoy was sent to the consulate because of the increase in border violence. Mexican authorities were holding a "John Doe." Dick used all of his consular instincts to first establish that the man was American, since he had no documentation. The man was a 50 or 60-year-old black man who was picked up in Nuevo Laredo as a vagrant. He claimed he had walked there from Honduras. Other than that, no further information.

On a hunch, McCoy started naming Vietnamese towns and villages. "Khe Sanh bad place." John Doe said. In the end, border officials accepted our affidavit stating John Doe was an American and the psychiatric ward in Laredo,

Texas took custody of him while the consulate started working with Veterans Affairs to get an ID. Then, against all assurances to McCoy, the Texas hospital prescribed "Greyhound therapy." They put John Doe on a bus and sent him north to Cleveland, another place he had mentioned.

You might think diplomatic events are receptions heavy with hors d'oeuvres and champagne, but the Cabalgata was a typical border annual diplomatic event. It was a horseback ride along the Rio Grande, or Rio Bravo as they say on the Mexican side. Thousands of people and horses participate, and I joined in.

My horse was "Comanche," a slight horse, but he looked fine. I had been on some Cuban horses that were so big and powerful you just could not rein them in when they wanted to gallop. I talked to Comanche's owner and asked if I could take him for a ride the night before the event. The owner agreed. I hopped on, I didn't worry too much that the stirrups were a little out of reach, I figured I'd get the horse set up perfectly in the morning. The reins didn't close in a circle of leather either as I was used to, but rather had two leather strands, one on each side. There were a lot of extra strips of leather too. I was unfamiliar with this set-up, so I just balled the strands up in my fist and took off. Comanche seemed nervous but I got him to trot and then gallop. My cowboy hat flew off and I circled back to get it. One of the caballeros from the ranch picked it up and handed it to me, just brushing Comanche's withers with it.

He took off like he was being whipped and headed straight toward a metal gate. The gate was too high to jump. If he hit it at that speed he could die and I'd be crushed. I bailed out at the last second, not able to rein him in because my feet didn't have a good purchase on the stirrups. I hit the ground hard. Comanche eased up and just missed the fence.

I stayed up in my tent that night in lots of pain and learned that the reins *were* designed to whip the horse. Since I balled up the reins, Comanche thought I was going to whip him any second. That's why he took off when he felt the hat, he thought that was the start of the whipping.

I got back on the horse in the morning, having learned my lesson, and went at a slow, painful walking pace. I saw one horse die from the heat. I didn't make the whole trail ride, that would go on for another couple of days. I headed home. Kathy said she had never seen anyone as black, blue, and purple as me. My body looked like one big bruise.

Several months later the owners invited me to their ranch to ride one of their racehorses around the property. I took care to make sure the reins were right, the stirrups set, the cinch just tight enough. No more rushing off half prepared. It was glorious.

Things are about to get heavy, so let me pause with some of the good things. Real Mexican food. Not Tex-Mex, not Taco Bell, but the real thing is delicious, if challenging in terms of spice. The real border hands would bring their own peppers in envelopes to a restaurant and put their peppers in the food. Man. Kathy said sometimes it was so hot she just wanted to get up from the table and run around to cool off!

Another good thing… horseback riding with Kalia. This was one of my favorite father-daughter things. Kalia would grab some of her friends on the Texas side where she went to school and we'd ride along the Rio Grande, enjoying the peace and quiet, the birds, and the dash back to the ranch when we turned around. It is hard to imagine a wall along that beautiful stretch of river. We always followed up with a smoothie at a local place and it was a nice Sunday ritual. And volleyball with the guards. I lived in the compound and we played after work all the time. We had some great rallies and lots of fun.

But back to Consulate Nuevo Laredo business. Those same guards came through when we spotted a child in a car seat in 110-degree weather with all the windows rolled up and the doors locked. I ordered them to smash the window and let air into the car. The parents later wanted the consulate to pay for the damage. No.

The next exhumation, or attempt anyway, was based on a tip called in about a missing American presumed murdered. The Mexican authorities thought they knew the location and they asked for an American police dog. I got an American team from across the river to agree and we went to the abandoned ranch. Inside the house we found a false trapdoor under the toilet that led to a basement, but that wasn't where the dog alerted. The dog smelled something in the corral. The Mexican authorities brought shovels and the guys went to work. In no time we found a watch. Then the diggers claimed the ground was too hard and it was impossible for there to be a body underneath. This was a Mexican operation, we were there to support, so we reluctantly called off the dog. I imagine the dog was right and the diggers were told they would be killed if they found something. Another dog died in his car when the border patrol "forgot" about him. Again, my guess is that the cartel had a bounty out for the dog due to his effectiveness in finding drugs.

We did have wins. Some with the help of Mexican officials. And I should say on the Texas side of the border that Mexico had extremely good consular officials, good diplomats and good people who cared about looking out for their Mexican nationals lost in the desert or in prison. They were doing the same job as us five miles away on the Mexican side. The only difference was that while we were dealing with dozens of Americans, they dealt with hundreds of Mexicans.

We cooperated through the Border Liaison Mechanism (BLM) which had regular meetings chaired by the two consuls. We would get the mayors, police chiefs and border officials together and set times for the international bridges and share intelligence and just work things out like neighbors. Relations with other federal agencies were good. The FBI and the U.S. Marshalls were always ready to share information and the Secret Service would always let us know when President Bush's girls were in our consular district partying with friends on the Mexican side.

Several cases required creativity on both sides. My deputy, Joe DeMaria felt his antennae go up when a middle-aged man showed up at the consulate with his 14-year-old "niece." The man seemed uncomfortable and the relationship didn't seem easy and familial. Joe checked the databases and found the man was wanted in New Jersey for sex with minors.

We went to the Mexican authorities, figuring it would be a quick arrest and deportation. Instead, the Chief of Police said, "It's not a crime in Mexico. Living with a 14-year-old girl. It's bad, but it's no crime."

"So what do we do?"

"Nothing, go play tennis."

I didn't say anything. Shocked. There was a long pause. He said, "You say the Marshals want him?"

"Yes, and I want him out of here too and the girl protected."

"Let me see what I can do," the Chief said.

Soon after we were back in touch. I sat in the Chief's office.

"Bad news for your American. He needs a residency permit if he wants to stay in Mexico. He needs a permit after Day 12 of his stay here. He can only get that at the Mexican Consulate on the Texas side. If you want, we'll pick him up, drive him to the international bridge and you can walk him over to Laredo to apply for the residency card. Be at customs at 2 p.m. And by the way, my aunt needs a visa."

No promises, but as a very experienced consul general once told me, "I lost my virginity over visas a long time ago." Sometimes, the greater good is an element in decision-making.

At five after two I was walking across the bridge with our suspect. He was a big man, but big in the way someone is who sits in front of a computer for too long. At mid-bridge a hand took him firmly by the arm.

The U.S. Marshal asked for his identity. He gave it.

"Please come with my partner and me."

The man's head dropped, and he walked quietly to the other side of the bridge with the two very tall men with shoulder pistols under their jackets. The suspect never looked back at me.

Despite the press of American citizen services, we did do some public diplomacy. For the 150th anniversary of the consulate we invited the ambassador to come and give remarks. He was actually our second choice. I wrote to Texas author Larry McMurtry to see if he could come, knowing that he understood Western history better than anyone. I was a big fan of *Lonesome Dove*. Mr. McMurtry answered, saying, alas, he did not do public events anymore. I tried to work "alas" into as many of my writings as possible after that.

Every post had a special family activity. In Mexico, it was riding horses along the Rio Grande or "Rio Bravo."

STEP 14 – DO THE RIGHT THING
(still Nuevo Laredo, Mexico)

It sounds stranger than fiction, but one American couple, in a drug- and alcohol-induced haze, tried to sell their infant in the downtown square in Nuevo Laredo. Someone made an anonymous report and the parents were picked up and put in jail and the child taken to Mexican Child Services. Mexican authorities could not get anyone to testify, although we found many eyewitnesses that corroborated the anonymous tip. The infant, with blonde hair and blue eyes, was clearly in danger with those two. We picked her up from the Mexican Child Protection Service and headed to the border to take her to Child Protective Services in Texas, since she was an American.

Just as we were at Mexican Customs, I'm told, the parents were being released from jail. By all rights, once they were free, they would have to be reunited with the girl, as the parents had no charges pending. Somehow, we didn't get the call that they were free from jail until we were on the other side of the river. Darn cell phones just don't work on the border sometimes. We placed the girl in the protective custody of the state of Texas. The parents would have to convince a judge that they were fit to get her back. They never appeared in court. The last I heard the child was with a new loving Texas family and doing well.

Another child, who had taken a wrong turn in life, was not doing as well but she was doing her best to survive. We got a report from a young runaway boy that his sister, also a runaway, was in the custody of narcos in a downtown house in Nuevo Laredo. He took us by the hideout at night and we reported the details to Nuevo Laredo police, making sure to get the teenage boy taken care of on the Texas side where his mom drove from Louisiana to pick him up. We kept after the police for news on the missing girl for a couple of weeks.

Then a call woke me up around one in the morning. (If you are going to go into the Foreign Service, especially as a consular officer, be sure to train yourself to wake up fully when the phone rings.)

It was the prosecutor's office. Our missing teenage girl, we'll call her Syndi, was in the police station. We needed to come to the procuracy to pick her up.

Deputy Consul General Joe DeMaria and I went to the station. We sat and listened to her as the prosecutor took her statement.

"So you have no description of the men who held you? How is that?" The prosecutor spoke in heavily accented English. He was in his thirties. Nicely dressed. Not overweight. Maybe somebody from Mexico City. He struck me as a bit too smooth for the border.

"I don't know, they were just regular guys, you know. Thirty or something. They were old!" Syndi's hands slid under her legs. Her eyes were unfocused. She shifted in her chair. She threw back her dirty blonde hair.

"I really need a cigarette." She looked pleadingly at the prosecutor. He nodded toward the courtyard.

There Syndi leaned over the railing, looking into the dark courtyard below. The building was typical old Spanish style with interior offices and a central courtyard below. In this case, the courtyard served as a parking lot, and our white consulate Suburban sat in a corner.

"So," Syndi took a deep drag, her fingers shaking. "They told me this afternoon what to say. And…" She looked around quickly, "The guys that were holding me, they are the ones who are here. You'll see. The big one. He keeps checking on me. Every time he walks in the room I jump. I think I'm going to pass out or something. I can't breathe when he comes in."

Joe and I listened. So they fed her a line to tell the "investigator," while the gang members, also known as Nuevo Laredo Police officers, were intimidating her. They wanted to be sure she said nothing before crossing into the U.S. No one would be taking this case further, so we didn't know what the show was for. Obviously, it was for our benefit. We went back in.

The questioning dragged on. It was almost 3 a.m. and I was tired.

The big man came in to glare at Syndi every few minutes. She was rapidly deteriorating.

The prosecutor continued unfazed by the obvious dynamics. "So, the address where they held you, you don't know it. How is that?" The prosecutor cocked his head to the side.

I stood up.

"That's it. That's enough. Look, she's not a suspect, she's not under arrest. We're going. Let's go, Syndi."

I grabbed her arm and spun her on her heels, and we walked out. Joe followed. We arrived in the courtyard. We hopped in the Suburban. Joe in the driver seat, me shotgun, Syndi in the back seat.

Joe put the car in gear and the huge wooden doors from the courtyard to the street closed. Ten policemen surrounded the car. No one pulled a gun, but guns and the threat were very real.

For two minutes no one said a word. Then a small man in a black jumpsuit with the big man in tow approached the car. "Get out little girl." He tapped the glass lightly. Smiled. He kept tapping. I told her to stay put. On both sides of the car police were yelling at us to get out. I rolled down my window two inches. Enough to talk.

"You are violating the Vienna Convention. We have a right to consular access, and you have no right to our vehicle." I said.

"Just give us the girl. We'll take her across the border. It's procedure. And we'll turn her over to you. You have no right to walk out of a criminal investigation. This girl was kidnapped. It's serious. We have serious questions for her."

"There is no procedure and there is no reason why she can't go with us to the border. She is not a criminal."

"It's our procedure. You can't violate it. Just give us the girl."

"No."

On Joe's side of the car another conversation was taking place.

"Open the lock. Just give us the girl. Then we'll let you go on your way."

"Oh yea, blow me pal. Fuck off." Joe was more direct than I was.

I almost laughed. Here I was discussing the Vienna Convention and Joe was telling them to fuck off. Very diplomatic! I noticed my legs were shaking. I got out my cell and dialed the State Department's operations center. Ops answered immediately.

"Hostage might be too strong a word, but here's the situation..." I outlined our situation. Fifteen minutes later ops called back and told us that the anti-terrorist team was being spun up.

I dialed another number and got hold of Dick McCoy, our retired, razor sharp consular officer. Dick got hold of a Mexican undercover narcotics officer. In 15 minutes the undercover agent was on the scene, brokering a deal.

Showing up that night blew his cover. He had been assigned to Nuevo Laredo to keep watch. If a major cartel kingpin showed up the agent was to call Mexico City, to ask for further orders from on high. Now, that capability would go up in smoke. There was no one left to trust on the border. Not even the army high command, since their elite counter narcotics team had already gone to the dark side to become the Zetas, the new breed of violent cartel gang.

The agent was in his windbreaker. He was the ultimate low-profile professional, but tonight he was visible and vulnerable. He worked quickly and quietly. He identified the leader. He made two calls on his cell phone. Five minutes later it was game over and we were rolling out of the courtyard toward the border. Syndi was sobbing in the back seat. She had a lot on her mind.

Me too. Was it worth it to give the agent up? What did he give up in return for our safe release? Should we have stayed at the police station to let the charade of Syndi's questioning go on?

We told Ops Center to stand down.

The next morning I got a call from the Chief of the Border Patrol. "You know your friend from last night, the little girl Syndi? Well, she escaped from our detention at 6 a.m. We caught her again a couple of hours later trying to cross into Nuevo Laredo. She was so desperate to get some cocaine back into her system she was ready to be their little love slave again. We're driving her all the way to Port Arthur, Louisiana now and the authorities and her mom can lock her up and figure out what to do with her."

"Syndi" was lucky and would get a second chance.

Another girl, local high schooler Sylvia Solis, ran out of luck.

We heard that Sylvia was missing so we talked to the local police, entered her information into our databases and hoped she'd show up somewhere in Mexico. We talked to downtown merchants. We had one photo of Sylvia that we showed around. She was in a car, smiling, full of life, young, and beautiful. I'll never forget it. She was 17, a little older than my daughter. Maybe she ran off with a boyfriend? What else could we do to find her? I couldn't think of anything.

Then I got a call. It was from an impeccable source that I still can't reveal. The caller said that Sylvia and a man from Laredo had been kidnapped and killed and were buried in the backyard of a drug dealer in Nuevo Laredo.

I was mad. Narco violence was bad, but until then innocent teens – and by all accounts Sylvia was innocent – were not targeted. She happened to be in the company of a Mr. Villagomez, who was in the drug trade, but they were not boyfriend and girlfriend.

I got on the phone with the appropriate state official and threatened to have him fired if we didn't get access to the yard. The minister hemmed and hawed and I dug in further saying the ambassador would be meeting with President Fox and item No. 1 would be getting these Americans home to their families.

"And the person responsible for holding things up would be you."

It was a total bluff. I was quite willing to do that but hadn't taken that step yet. I was insistent that the cartels were not going to murder an American citizen and walk away. The order came down that we could go to the backyard.

There were already rumors that the house would be booby trapped and yet my Foreign Service National employee, who got to the house first, was one of the first through the door. I got there a few minutes later, having driven from the Texas side. Coming through the cordon of police and soldiers it was one of the most heavily armed locations I had ever been in. Mexican Army heavy vehicles encircled the property and the streets for blocks. There were soldiers all over the place. I went through the house to the backyard. Inside it was faux, rich with paintings of white tigers and Aztec women.

Outside there were spotlights rigged up and the men shoveling knew exactly where to dig. It wasn't long until we could smell death. The minister came over to me and whispered just how bad this would be for him and for me. I didn't care.

Then, they had done their job; both bodies were on the ground. Villagomez was a big man. An autopsy revealed he had been buried alive. Sylvia was naked, the trauma to her body was obvious and infuriating. She had lost all of her hair. In the morgue her mother could not be sure if she was her daughter and she had second thoughts even after her daughter was buried, holding out some hope that it wasn't her. I went home and disposed of the clothes I had on. I wished I could burn them. The smell of death permeated everything.

Mrs. Solis came regularly to the consulate. To his credit, the Mexican prosecutor came every time she requested it. And every single time he answered our questions the same way.

"Are there any suspects?"

"No."

"Are there any leads?"

"No."

And on the U.S. side the answers were "no" as well. Mrs. Solis tried to get video-tapes of the cars crossing at the international bridges, to see if the kidnappers were already in the car when they crossed from Laredo, Texas to Nuevo Laredo, Mexico. In those days, crossing the bridge to eat dinner, go to a bar, or to shop, was no big deal. But the tapes were not forthcoming, and Mrs. Solis continued to seek justice.

There is some solace in having brought their bodies back home to their families. Many go missing and are never recovered. The sad thing is they were just two casualties in what had become a war. I often wondered if Sylvia Solis had been a blonde "Spring Breaker" if the national media might not have focused on her case. Even the *San Antonio Express News* declined to print a story when I told their border reporter that Sylvia was missing. Dick McCoy learned through his sources that every gang member involved in the kidnapping and murder of Sylvia and Villagomez died hard.

I hope so.

Q: *Did you actually enjoy this job?*

ARMBRUSTER: What a great question. That was certainly a low point, seeing a mom crushed. But I felt like I was doing my job. I saw her every time she came to the consulate to meet with Mexican officials and I felt like that was a service that I was happy to provide, trying to work for her and other families who were affected by the drug violence. So, in terms of being a diplomat and providing a service and doing something that made a difference to people in their lives, yeah, I think a tour on the border fulfilled that requirement. It was satisfying and rewarding. When you help out an American in prison, that feels good.

Q: *What were your numbers per year, let's say, of applicants?*

ARMBRUSTER: It would be hard for me to give you a number except we were right up there with the busiest posts in the world. Tens of thousands of interviews.

Q: *And these were mostly visitor visas or a fair amount of immigrants as well.*

ARMBRUSTER: Then people would send their kids across to Laredo to go to school and you know there is just a lot of back and forth, just normal travel. The refusal rate wasn't terribly high. I don't know what it was, but you know we have workers, businessmen, students, we had just about everybody. Certainly family, but a lot of people would just cross to go shopping and then go back. Until 9/11 it was very easy… five minutes to cross the border. "Are you an American citizen?" "Yes." "Have a nice day."

Q: *You arrived in Nuevo Laredo in what year?*

ARMBRUSTER: We arrived in 2000.

Q: *OK so you had a solid year of work before 9/11. How did 9/11 change things for you?*

ARMBRUSTER: Everything. President Bush and President Fox were very close to an immigration agreement before 9/11 happened. That was going to reform the system and make it easier for many Mexicans to travel to the U.S., work seasonally, and go back home, because most people want to do that. They want to work and then go back and see their families. That whole effort was ended. The border crossings that had been so easy - really you just present yourself at the border and state your citizenship and off you go - became a nightmare. It just became hours and hours. Sometimes I would ride my bike across the border because I didn't want to spend a few hours in the car. We got a little apartment on the Laredo side so my wife could work at the library in Laredo and my daughter could go to school, because it was just untenable to get up at 4 a.m. to get to school at 8 a.m. They did that for a while. Then finally they would get through the checkpoint and they would go to Denny's or someplace and have breakfast, and it was a madhouse.

Q: *Alright, so to go back, in addition to all of the consular work you also had commercial work. Did NAFTA,*[14] *or the NAFTA councils that were created, were you involved with those or how did you interact with NAFTA things?*

ARMBRUSTER: On a retail basis let's say, I would go to the Caterpillar plant on the Mexican side. There they had a program called "pay for work; pay for knowledge." So, the people advanced in the Caterpillar plant based on the training they took; if they decided to learn English, they could move up quicker. If they decided to take another advanced course they would move up. Which was different from the U.S. system which was based on seniority. So, it was interesting to see how Mexican-American companies were a good thing. It just seemed very promising. We worked on transportation issues, coordinating bridge closures for example. For a while we were the warehouse for goods going to Mexico City for American diplomats and their families. That later moved to Matamoros. But we had a big role in that shipping the first year. As far as NAFTA goes, we were just seeing a very busy, productive border, but we also knew that the drug smuggling and illegal crossing was a fact of life and a real feature of life on the border.

Q: *Now one of the perennial issues in NAFTA even after it was approved, was the issue of trucking, Mexican trucking going into the U.S., safety issues and environmental issues. Did you end up having to work on that?*

ARMBRUSTER: No, the embassy would have worked on that, but I certainly saw the sense in allowing Mexican drivers to be able to take their trucks all the way to their destination and back and I think some of the rumblings about the drivers being unsafe frankly struck me as racist. Globalization is the free movement of capital and goods and it should also include labor, so talent goes where it is needed. NAFTA was trying to address that. We had the move-

---

[14]   North American Free Trade Agreement.

ment of goods and capital, but the movement of labor is still a sticking point.

Q: So as Consul General there is Nuevo Laredo the city, but you have a consular district that extends beyond. Were there issues related to that?

ARMBRUSTER: The Laughlin Air Force Base is in Del Rio, right across from Ciudad Acuña, so sometimes we had cross border issues. Our consular agent assisted in a traffic accident on the Mexican side involving our airmen, for example. We also had a consular agent in Piedras Negras and we visited Americans in three prisons in our consular district.

We would travel a bit and I drove with my deputy to Mexico City. It was safe enough to do that then, and that was the most beautiful ride I have ever taken along the TransAmerica highway. Mexico is just a gorgeous place. The food is great. And it's so rich. A Japanese businessman once said if Japan had Mexico's land and resources it would rule the world. I enjoyed speaking the language and I enjoyed my colleagues, so it was a good tour. I do look at it fondly, but I will never forget the cases of violence and the threats.

Q: Culturally they say that the northern area, say 100 miles to the U.S. border, is distinct from the rest of Mexico in a variety of ways. Did you get that feeling as well?

ARMBRUSTER: When you travel around Mexico a little bit you really get a feel for indigenous areas and other areas, especially along the border where it really is a Tex-Mex environment, and then Mexico City with its great cultural heritage and the pyramids, there's a lot of history. It is a marvelously diverse country. So when you think of Mexico and the coastline and the mountains it has an awful lot to offer.

Q: Any indigenous issues while you were there?

ARMBRUSTER: The black American soldiers, many Civil War veterans, moved to Mexico and married into indigenous families. That is interesting history, the Buffalo Soldiers.[15] It is a colorful area with the Texas Rangers and the Comanches who ruled that region for decades. You can almost feel it. You look at the scenery and you can just imagine an Indian on horseback. It is a striking place.

Q: *Now I imagine with this level of responsibility you are now an 0-1.*

ARMBRUSTER: I was promoted to 01 in Nuevo Laredo.

Q: *Before you move on to the Naval War College just one more sort of general question. In this period where you were the Consul General and head of a reasonable-sized consulate how did you learn leadership issues? Did you get training or what would you say were the ways you took on new skills of leadership while you were running the place.*

ARMBRUSTER: I did take the training that FSI offered on leadership. I took negotiations training, but I think probably I learned the most from my staff and my deputy, Joe DeMaria. At one point he corrected me. We had taken a poll on some question - I don't remember what - and I didn't like the results of the poll. I had my own opinion of what we should do. Joe said, "Well what is the point of having a poll if you are not going to follow it?" I thought *You are right. OK, I will take one for the team.* If we are going to open it up to everybody, then you have to live with the results. So, I think I have always tried to be open and create an atmosphere where people could come to me and talk in a safe, no-consequences setting. I don't know if I always lived up to it, but I always felt communications have been pretty good in the missions I have been in.

---

15   https://www.history.com/topics/westward-expansion/buffalo-soldiers

I tried to foster that by listening to colleagues, especially local staff. I don't think I could ever say enough about the local staff we work with. One of the guys in Russia was actually a survivor of Chernobyl and he had a lifetime pass on the metro because of his going to the scene. We just work with terrific people all over the world. More often than not the local staff will tell you what they think because they are going to be there after we leave, and they have seen it all. If we are willing to learn from them, we can grow.

October 2003

Mexican Army deserters start war for control of border city

By Mark Stevenson / Associated Press

NUEVO LAREDO, Mexico – Members of an elite Mexican Army unit have deserted and formed a drug gang, using their military training to launch a violent battle for control of this border city, Mexico's top anti-drug prosecutor said in an interview with Associated Press.

The war for Nuevo Laredo is unlike other recent drug conflicts – it's a turf war involving most of Mexico's major cartels in broad alliances not seen in a decade. It has the Mexican Army fighting an organized unit of former comrades, and it has cost American lives.

'They are extremely violent, and they are very much feared in the region because of the bloodshed they unleash,' Jose Santiago Vasconcelos, Mexico's top anti-drug prosecutor, told AP.

The battles, which have taken 87 lives since 2002, have involved unprecedented alliances among Mexico's drug cartels, according to Nuevo Laredo police commander Martin Landa Herrera.

'I don't think anything like this has happened before in Mexico,' he said in an interview. 'I have never heard of this many cartels fighting for one piece of territory.'

Known as the 'Zetas' or 'Zs', the new drug gang – which appears to have won control of the city – is led by former members of an elite paratroop and intelligence battalion that was posted to the border state of Tamaulipas in the 1990s to fight drug traffickers.

Vasconcelos said about 31 of the estimated 350 members of the Special Air Mobile Force Group, posted to the border state of Tamaulipas in the 1990s, had deserted and joined the drug turf war.

'They have high-powered weapons, training and intelligence capabilities,' Landa Herrera said of the Zetas, whose name comes from the radio code word designating a police commander. 'They have even tapped our radio communications. They listen in on us.'

The Defense Department has refused to confirm any of its soldiers formed the Zetas. But the army recently began posting wanted posters across the country offering rewards for the deserters, some still pictured in army uniforms. That led to speculation the soldiers were behind the Zetas.

The skirmishing began in 2001 as a dispute among local drug gangs that operated with the permission of reputed Gulf drug cartel leader Osiel Cardenas. By early 2002, the battle had heated up enough that the Zetas appeared, working as hitmen for Cardenas in a bid to restore order.

But Cardenas' arrest [on] March 14 during a shootout in the nearby border city of Matamoros opened the floodgates for a wider conflict. With Cárdenas in jail, cartels across Mexico – Michoacán, Ciudad Juárez, Sinaloa, and possibly Tijuana – sensed weakness and tried to move in on the territory.

Escaped Sinaloa drug lord Joaquin 'El Chapo' Guzman reportedly allied himself with the Juarez cartel, sending in gunmen to take over Nuevo Laredo. At the same time, another local trafficker tried to form an alliance with the Valencia cartel, based in the western state of Michoacán. And police even arrested a mid-level operator for the Tijuana-based Arellano Felix cartel in Nuevo Laredo.

Such alliances – and an all-out war between multiple cartels – haven't been seen since the wars between Mexican gangs in the late 1980s and early 1990s.

'We're seeing these alliances, but this is just proof of the crisis these gangs are in,' Vasconcelos said. 'There is no one single group strong enough anymore to dominate the territory.'

The Zetas do appear to have the upper hand and are still linked to Cardenas, city police say. While dozens of hired gunslingers from other cartels have died, Vasconcelos said only a few Zetas have been killed and only one or two have been captured.

The Zetas have killed dozens of rival traffickers, trading shots from passing sport utility vehicles on the streets of Nuevo Laredo. In one attack, they engaged in a shootout in broad daylight just yards from where the city's mayor was attending a flag-raising ceremony.

The Zetas sometimes leave their victims' bodies packed in car trunks. In one massacre, they wrote information about a rival gang on a wall above a pile of victims, encouraging police to dismantle the other group.

Nobody has to tell Houston resident Noe Villarreal how vicious the war has become. On Sept. 27, a commando of at least 30 masked men carrying assault rifles kidnapped his brother – Hayward, Calif., businessman Juan Villarreal Garcia – from his Mexico home in Sabinas Hidalgo, a town south of Nuevo Laredo.

The gunmen had fanned out across the town in search of a rival. They killed two policemen, kidnapped seven people, burst into Villarreal's home – in a possible case of mistaken identity – and dragged the 78-year-old tortilla-store owner away.

The other hostages were released soon afterward, but Villarreal remains missing and is presumed dead. The area is so violent that nobody is sure who kidnapped him or why.

'I don't know if it was the Zetas,' said Noe Villarreal, 'because the Zetas have never released anyone alive. That's not their style.'

It wouldn't be the first time that Americans have died in the conflict.

A wild pre-dawn battle on Aug. 1 in Nuevo Laredo left at least three dead – one of them a man from Laredo, Texas – and six wounded. Police and army troops exchanged fire with cars believed to be carrying drug traffickers.

The three were killed when their SUV exploded after police bullets hit the vehicle's gas tank.

And in June 2001, a couple from Laredo, Texas, – Sylvia Solis and Juan Villagomez – were kidnapped by drug traffickers, although it is unclear why. She was raped and strangled. He was beaten and buried alive.

———

As if the narco violence didn't keep us busy enough, Joe also figured out that something fishy was going on with visas. We had outreach teams travel from Nuevo Laredo to Piedras Negras and Ciudad Acuña to interview visa applicants that otherwise might not make the trip to the consulate. It was a good consular service. But Joe noticed that the visa issuances were higher than the appointments. When someone makes an appointment, they get prescreened to see if there were previous denials, criminal convictions, etc. So, one of our visa adjudicators had a business on the side for people who wouldn't make it through prescreening.

This was serious business, as people getting visas could be anyone, cartel members, terrorists, you name it. Joe wrote a memo to Diplomatic Security and they came into town under cover. At first, everyone was a suspect, including me. They followed me when I went over the bridge to the Texas side. Finally, I said to the diplomatic security agents, "Look guys, I want you to make this bust as badly as you do. That hidden camera you plan to put in Window 1 on Monday? That's not going to work, because Mike, your main suspect, is working at Window 3 on Monday. We rotate adjudicators so people in the waiting room can't say, 'you want to go to Window whatever, he's easy.'" They installed the camera in Window 3. From then we worked well together; I just wished they could hurry before more damage was done. But it was a long investigation.

Finally, DS was ready. They asked if they could bring guns to put in our vault just in case things went bad. I said ok. They locked us down and no one was allowed in or out of the consulate. Mike was arrested on the Texas side. Everyone in the consulate was interviewed. We fired the entire guard force, because they were directing applicants to Mike. We went from being the third busiest consulate in the world to doing zero visas.

Mike went to jail. He was not a Foreign Service Officer. We had civil service adjudicators along the border, mostly bilingual men and women from the local community. Unfortunately, they had many ties to the people they were interviewing, and it was hard to be dispassionate and not be compromised. Maybe impossible.

I don't know if it was letting the guards go, but I received a death threat not long after Mike's arrest. It was a simple email, a photo of a dead body on a gurney. The email just read Happy New Year.

I was also threatened after I had a policeman reassigned. A young woman came to the consulate and told us that a local policeman raped her and forced her to draw money from an ATM. We could not get the authorities to prosecute without witnesses or evidence. I lobbied the mayor to have the policeman disciplined.

The policeman was sent to the south of Mexico for a year. When he got back to Nuevo Laredo, he spotted me. He was boiling mad. He yelled at me. I listened. I could tell he was on the point of exploding. I stayed calm, didn't yell back. Then I took a gamble. I turned my back and walked away.

I don't know how close I was to being in real trouble, but I suspect very, very close. Some days in Nuevo Laredo could be extremely stressful. Lots of long days and midnight calls. I took to taking 15-minute naps in my office just closing the door and laying on the couch. Fifteen minutes did the trick. I'd be asleep, dream, and be right back up.

I worked one presidential visit. President Bush came to Monterrey, Mexico with Secretary of State Colin Powell. I did have an elevator moment with them, going from the garage to the first floor, but elevator speech had not yet been invented. I considered introducing myself and telling them things were getting bad on the border and that the violence could spread to U.S. cities and towns, engulfing small police stations and becoming like the border, but the elevator ride was a short one floor and I couldn't compose the speech quickly enough. I did need more seasoning! So I escorted them to a hold room, which seemed to make Secretary Powell grumpy, but they were soon released to do their thing.

The president came to Mexico with a new message on the U.S. approach to global poverty, pledging to increase our assistance and committing to open markets:

> *The lesson of our time is clear: When nations close their markets and opportunity is hoarded by a privileged few, no amount — no amount — of development aid is ever enough. When nations respect their people, open markets, invest in better health and education, every dollar of aid, every dollar of trade revenue and domestic capital is used more effectively. We must tie greater aid to political and legal and economic reforms. And by insisting on reform, we do the work of compassion. The United States will lead by example. I have proposed a 50-percent increase in our core development assistance over the next three budget years. Eventually, this will mean a $5-billion annual increase over current levels. These new funds will go into a new Millennium Challenge Account, devoted to projects in nations that govern justly, invest in their people and encourage economic freedom. We will promote development from the bottom up, helping citizens find the tools and training and technologies to seize the opportunities of the global economy.*[16]

The shame of President Bush's presidency was that just as he was reaching out to President Fox to fix the immigration issues between our countries 9/11 happened. Bush wanted to find a way for Mexicans to live and work in the U.S.

---

[16] Remarks by President George W. Bush to the UN international conference on financing for development. https://www.pbs.org/newshour/politics/white_house-jan-june02-bush_03-22

legally and to adjust the status of those in the U.S., without penalizing people seeking legal immigration. Once 9/11 happened his initiative was derailed.

On September 11, Joe and I were in Eagle Pass. I saw the planes crash on the news and knew immediately what it was. I had a dream that morning that I was interviewing Bin Laden for the State Department. He was in custody somewhere and it was my job to talk to him, just like I might talk to an American prisoner. I remember the sense of violence. He was not a household name yet, but we knew he was responsible for the embassy bombing in Nairobi. I think I must have seen the news and gone back to sleep and had the dream, but it's possible I had it that morning and it was just coincidental that 9/11 happened that same morning. In any case, Joe and I were on the Texas side and needed to get back to the consulate. We talked about flying in a small plane from Eagle Pass, but we were told we'd be likely to be shot down. So we drove back and the world, and especially the border, was different. I asked my Mexican colleague and friend Consul Hernandez-Joseph when things would calm down and get back to normal. He said, "This is the new normal." What had been a soft border became a lot harder.

Near the end of our tour I decided to take a little break from Mexico and go to Afghanistan on a temporary duty tour. I volunteered to cover for a Political Officer so he could go home for Christmas.

STEP 15 – DO A TDY TOUR
Kabul, Afghanistan December 2002–January 2003

Coming into Kabul Airport I could see a field littered with Russian planes. Pick up at the airport was fast. We were in the car about as soon as they confirmed my identity. There wasn't much chit chat. The man riding shotgun got on the radio, "Three minutes out." A few more minutes and he said, "30 seconds out." The gate lifted and we were in the compound. Despite the introduction to heavy security, December 2002 was actually a more permissive time in Afghanistan.

My hooch,[17] a container converted into a bedroom, was fine. The air was not fine. It was smoky from all the diesel engines burning in the city. I had a hard time with it, but the medical unit fixed me up and I was in business.

I traveled to mosques and talked to imams. One of them, a man in his 70s, invited me in for tea. We sat on the floor with our tea and he described the U.S. presence this way:

> You are like the Afghan story of the destroying mouse. A mouse gets into your house. Your neighbor says, 'I will help, I will kill the mouse.' But the neighbor takes a sledgehammer and room by room searches for the mouse, destroying every room as he goes. He says he is helping you, but he is destroying you. That is you. The terrorists are the mouse. They are not that big a problem. And they are our problem. That was the Russians too. At least you pretend you want to be friends. The Russians were just brutal.

It was an eye-opening view. We traveled throughout the city in an unarmored van. It was just me, a driver, and an interpreter who I hope at some point got a visa to go to the U.S. Sometimes we would get hard stares from young men, usually we passed unnoticed.

The only violence I witnessed, aside from our driver ramming another car out of the way, was from the embassy courtyard. There is a flag with a monument stone for Ambassador Dubs, who was assassinated when the Soviets rolled in. We would hang out near the flag when we wanted to take a break. I was there

---

[17] Thatched hut or improvised living space.

with four or five officers and at the apartment building across the street someone opened fire on an American A-10 plane with an AK-47. The plane was flying with real attitude and we could just imagine the pilot waiting for an order to return fire. It never came. The military higher ups must have figured shooting at an apartment building in downtown Kabul would not be a good idea. The A-10 peeled off and flew away.

Just before that I said, "Hey, if we can see the guy shooting, that means he can see us. He only needs to swing the rifle our way and we're done. Let's go back in." We did.

The vehicle ramming took place on the way to Bagram Air Base to pick up a VIP. On the way back a car got too close to the embassy vehicle. The embassy driver casually hit the offending car, moved it out of the way, destroying the fender in the process and we proceeded. Seemed like good training to me on the part of the driver.

There was already a feeling in the embassy that Afghanistan was going to be overshadowed by the war clouds developing over Iraq. Everyone in the mission felt like the full weight of the American effort had not yet been brought to bear in Afghanistan, and that any diversion would weaken the effort. One officer in Greece resigned in protest of the Iraq War, but there was no defining dissent cable that caused Washington to take stock and change course.

Over the years, State has certainly had experts that Washington should listen to. People like Ryan Crocker with deep experience in crisis countries who could see the multiple dimensions of military engagement. He was solid while ambassador in Afghanistan about ten years after my one month stay in 2002. After a 20-hour attack by militants on the embassy he said it was "no big deal," and just showed the weakness and desperation of the militants. Crocker was always coolness and calm deliberation under fire.

This really is not a very big deal, a hard day for the embassy and my staff, who behaved with enormous courage and dedication, but half a dozen RPG rounds from 800 meters away – that isn't Tet, that's harassment," he said in reference to the Viet Cong offensive during the Vietnam war. "If that's the best they can do, I think it's actually a statement of their weakness and, more importantly, since Kabul is in the hands of Afghan security, it's a real credit to the Afghan national security forces.

The Guardian, September 14, 2011

At about this time I was bidding on my next assignment. The Political Chief job in Oslo was open and given my Arctic, Russian, and Finnish experience it seemed a good fit. It was. Embassy Oslo determined I was their top choice. Then, another bidder, a staffer from the 7th floor, decided he wanted Oslo. I was told to look elsewhere.

When I told my Career Development Officer, or CDA – also known as Career Destruction

Officer – about it, he said, "Well, where do you want to go?"

"You mean I can just tell you?"

"Well, when the system creates a situation like that, we try to make it right."

"OK," I said. "The War College."

He said, "Which one?"

Living near Annapolis most of my life I said, "The Naval War College in Newport."

"Let me see what I can do."

That assignment came through, along with a follow-on assignment as Deputy Chief of Mission to our embassy in Dushanbe, Tajikistan. I had called about another Central Asian post and spoke to Dick Hoagland, Ambassador-designate to Tajikistan. He said, "What about Tajikistan?"

"Tell me about it."

So, I had that lined up too to follow right after the War College. But while I was still in Kabul the ambassador in Norway was having second thoughts and wondered if I would go for the political job if he pushed it. I thought about my options and decided to stick with the War College and Tajikistan.

These crossroads in a Foreign Service career come up every two or three years. You have to decide which direction you want to go. For me, the guiding principle had been adventure, but I was beginning to see that the real value was in service. What you can do to make things better, to make a difference. I figured I could make more of a difference in Tajikistan, especially with additional training from the Naval War College.

STEP 16 – LEARN FROM YOUR MILITARY COLLEAGUES THE NAVAL WAR COLLEGE – Newport, Rhode Island 2003–2004

The Naval War College is mostly filled with warriors. Navy guys but also other services. I said at one point, "You know we civilians in the War College are like little grains of salt in a loaf of bread."

My professor said, "Yeah, but have you ever tasted bread without the salt? You need a little pinch!"

For the sailors, the War College was their chance to transition from pilots and Special Operators to more weighty Washington desk jobs. It's a tough transition when you are a field guy and enjoy getting out and doing things.

I took advantage of the amenities in Newport, swimming in the warm months, getting my sailing license and renting navy sailboats, and playing tennis and volleyball in the annual army-navy games.

I enjoyed the seminars, respected my military colleagues, and wrote a paper on U.S.-Russian nuclear cooperation, called *Actionable Intelligence* that the War College published. The one-year program led to a master's in security studies. Which was funny because in Nuevo Laredo I got a master's from St Mary's in San Antonio, working nights and on the weekend. That degree was on conflict resolution. So I had conflict resolution and plain old conflict covered. And of course the big conflict then was in Afghanistan.

Q: *Was the paper classified?*

ARMBRUSTER: It was not, no. I think it is still in their library in fact as a research paper.

Q: *Well just as an aid could you briefly summarize your findings?*

ARMBRUSTER: Sure. I concluded that investment in closer collaboration with the Russians in nuclear cooperation was in our national security interest. Unfortunately, I think the Russians themselves were just not in any mood to cooperate, so we both lost an opportunity, because when we were buying their highly enriched uranium and blending it down to low enriched and burning it in our nuclear plants, I think that was good for both sides. It is a shame.

———

STEP 17 – GET LANDLOCKED
Dushanbe, Tajikistan 2004–2006

We came to Tajikistan through Almaty, Kazakhstan with an overnight in a hotel. On the TV there was coverage of the Beslan school siege, the three days of terror and carnage in Russia, showing again that any normal place can become a scene of terror.

The embassy in Tajikistan was really just a house in a normal Dushanbe neighborhood. The staff had been visiting Dushanbe from Almaty for years because of the Tajik Civil War. Kathy was only the second spouse to come to the newly open 24/7 embassy. My first week or so I got violently ill. I passed out from dehydration and I was to be hit with bouts of this illness every few months. We did find some restaurants eventually that were good, although their English menus left something to be desired. There was "Watery Dinner of the Day" and "Fried Spit," for example.

ARMBRUSTER: Then I was DCM for Ambassador Dick Hoagland in Tajikistan. We were very much focused on regional integration so that the Tajiks and Afghans and Uzbeks and Kyrgyz could get along and play together better. The U.S. was building a bridge between Tajikistan and Afghanistan. So, I worked on that project by getting permissions, even trying to speed up the delivery of cement sometimes when they were diverted for other projects from other donors, like Iran. I put together a counter narcotics group from Tajikistan and we flew to Kabul for the first ever intelligence sharing. That was successful and continues today. We were very happy about that.

On a separate trip I took Tajiks to Kabul and Kunduz for business development. Of course, that had become more problematic as the security situation in Afghanistan has just never really resolved itself. Those were some of the highlights.

We loved hiking in Tajikistan. It is just a beautiful area. Pretty remote. I remember flying home for home leave, and we went from Dushanbe to Osh, Bishkek, Baku, London, and then home. So, it was like 30 hours of travel. But we saw the kids. They came to see us and visited. So, it was a good tour.

Q: Aside from working on the regional aspects, is there anything to say about the relationship between Tajikistan and Afghanistan with regard to ethnic terms, because Afghanistan has Tajiks, [while] Tajikistan has other tribes from Afghanistan. And you hear about that in the media periodically but never with regional clarity.

ARMBRUSTER: One of the real warriors against the Soviets was a man named Masoud who was called the Lion of Panjshir. He was instrumental in that war and the Tajiks had a very big stake. Masoud was killed on 9/11 by operatives posing as journalists. You can still see his picture on billboards in the region. Tajikistan was coming out of its own civil war, so we were working on stabilization and conflict mitigation with different nationalities, ethnicities, and tribes. Many of the Central Asian frontiers are artificial. You go to Uzbekistan and there are Tajiks. Central Asia is a melting pot of many ethnicities. They have got a lot of resources and it is a shame when you go to these borders and it is dead quiet. They should be busy active places of cultural and commercial exchange. The security situation was still not perfect at the time, but it was a lot better to the point where families were allowed to come. We had a car bombing so there were security concerns, but on the whole Tajikistan was moving in a positive direction.

Q: How would you look at Tajikistan today, would you still say that it is moving in a positive direction?

ARMBRUSTER: All of Central Asia is underperforming in terms of both regional and global integration. We had Defense Secretary Rumsfeld visit and talk to President Rahmonov about establishing a U.S. military base there. He asked me if I thought it was feasible. I did. But Rahmonov said no.

Q: *Still part of a near abroad. Alright. Looking back from a career point of view were there particular talents or skills that were required while you were there that were useful for you as you moved along?*

ARMBRUSTER: Yes. Ambassador Hoagland was pretty much focused on the policy. That meant that I was working on the management and consular issues. Hoagland was a public diplomacy officer and he was an expert at it, but it gave me the chance to lead in all these different areas. We were building a new embassy so that required a real push working with the Bureau of Overseas Buildings Operations (OBO) and Diplomatic Security. I had been Consul General in Nuevo Laredo so that was good, but Dushanbe was a real full scope embassy whereas Nuevo Laredo was primarily there for visas and American citizens. We also had visitors. We had Secretary of State Condoleezza Rice. We had Rumsfeld… I really liked serving as control officer because we could advance issues that had been stuck. So, putting the team in place and having the right people as site officers and making sure we were making the most of every visit is good leadership experience as well.

The work was good. Commissioning new border checkpoints that the U.S. paid for, working with the UN on post conflict projects, women's development, and basically feelgood diplomatic initiatives. I'm not sure I ever gained Ambassador Richard Hoagland's confidence. When there was a car bombing in downtown Dushanbe he rushed back from a conference in Uzbekistan. I felt like saying, "I got this," but it was his post and I was his deputy. Dick was an excellent political reporter and his cables were regularly cited in Washington as being insightful, timely, and funny. He could find the absurdity in the autocratic Tajik rule.

The ambassador allowed me to travel to Afghanistan twice. Once to start the first ever dialog between Tajik and Afghan intelligence officers. We took off in a C-130, spent a day trading information at a secure location and then our plane promptly broke down. With the Tajiks not sure of our motives it was the worst possible time for a malfunction, but the next day we flew safely home to Dushanbe and I know that the intelligence sharing continues to this day.

My initiative was "rewarded" with an Interior Ministry flight to look at border operations in an old Soviet-era helicopter. I've been in a lot of dodgy airplanes and helicopters, including the KrasAir (or Krash Air) plane with a "Chop Crash Axe Here" sign painted boldly on the fuselage, but that helicopter probably wins the prize as the scariest. It was so old it barely seemed airworthy.

My second trip to Afghanistan from Dushanbe was to promote business. I took Tajik businessmen to Kabul and Kunduz. Security had gotten tighter since my 2002 trip, but I was impressed with the young Afghan-Americans that I met trying to make a go of it in telecoms and other industries. They were hopeful and optimistic. Kunduz was a lovely small city. We stayed at a joint barracks nearby. One allied truck convoy in the region was attacked during our stay and a European serviceman was killed but we had no problems while in town and our welcome by the Afghans was hospitable and interested.

Secretary of State Condoleezza Rice came to Dushanbe and visited a girl's school. Like all VIP visits it was all highly scripted, but this advance team took it to a new level. Every advance team has "countdown meetings" to go over every step of this visit, but these guys wanted diagrams of every room of every meeting. I couldn't do it. My spatial and drawing skills were minimal and I felt like we were spending more time on minutiae than the actual visit. But it all came together.

Secretary of Defense Rumsfeld's visit was substantive, no diagrams, but neither was there the breakthrough he was looking for. He wanted to explore the idea of a U.S. base in Tajikistan, since the Kyrgyz were getting restless about hosting a base in their country as a supply point for Afghanistan. With Tajikistan right next door, it would be a good place for the proposed U.S. base. Rumsfeld asked me what I thought. I said I thought the Tajiks would go for it, needing money for their developing country and to offset Russia's outsized influence. I was wrong. The Tajik president told Secretary Rumsfeld that Russia simply wouldn't allow it and that a small country like Tajikistan was not as independent yet as they would like to be. Russia's influence was more than outsized, it was definitive on foreign policy questions, especially questions involving the U.S.

The "Great Game" in Central Asia that Alexander the Great played so well never ends. We visited one of the forts where Alexander is said to have wept because "There were no more worlds to conquer." Few people in Tajikistan would weep for Alexander, as he is seen as just another ruthless adventurer to sweep through their country.

On some of our trips upcountry in Tajikistan we would follow the Pyanj River. On one trip I spotted some kids swimming across the river from Tajikistan to Afghanistan. I asked that we stopped the car. The driver did. I looked long and hard and ran through the pluses and minuses of joining the kids for the swim from Tajikistan to Afghanistan. I finally decided no, and we went back to the embassy. Probably the right call and one of the few right calls involving me and water.

I also said "no" once when it was the wrong call. We were hurrying to a United Nations site for election monitoring. We were told if we didn't get there by dark the gates would shut, and we would not be let in. On the way we came across a terrible accident. The only person I could see was a woman whose legs were in the air and the car had jackknifed around her, effectively cutting her in half. It was impossible that she could have been alive. The driver asked, "Should we stop?"

I didn't see how we could have helped and said, "No." Quick decision, but wrong. Maybe we could have done some good. This was their country and I should have had the driver and bodyguard make the call. The UN could wait.

The drivers and bodyguards at the embassy were well disciplined and professional and had no doubt seen action in the Civil War. When the ambassador was away, I had the security detail. An advance car with guys with guns would arrive at my house, I'd get in the second car, and a follow car with more guys with guns, would be behind us. Then when the ambassador came back from his trip, I'd go back to riding my bike to and from the embassy.

Because we had no marine security guards, we divvied up the embassy emergency protection among ourselves, with the Regional Security Officer and his deputy taking one window, and our law enforcement guy and anyone else who could shoot taking the others. It felt like Fort Apache and there always seemed to be a security alert whenever the ambassador went out of town, prompting us to even close the embassy after one Emergency Action Committee meeting determined that the threat was real enough to take preventative action.

Kathy had a great librarian position with Quality Schools International and in the summer she helped with the pre-departure training for Tajik high school kids going to the U.S. to live with American families under State Department programs. They had a nice skit to get kids ready, comparing their expectations with the reality. In the expectations act they were greeted by name by the pilots, picked up at the airport by a loving American family with a huge SUV; they met Jennifer Lopez and the president, they had their own room in a grand suburban home, and they were the most popular kids in school. In the reality act the plane ride was long and cramped, the family was late coming to the airport, and they had to share a room with two siblings.

Kathy came home from one of the training sessions and it was almost like she had found a puppy. She showed me a picture of Manon Yusupov and basically asked, "Can we keep him?" Manny came back to the U.S. with us after Tajikistan for the year I had between Dushanbe and Vladivostok. He was the quietest kid I had ever met.

But little by little, Manny found himself through sports. He tried out as a kicker for the football team and then really excelled in wrestling. He was seconds away from making it to the Virginia state championships. Manny is now a diplomat himself with the Tajik Foreign Ministry with kids of his own. It was great to have him as an exchange student and I would recommend the State Department exchange programs to any family looking to be the host of an international student. It's a terrific way to learn about another culture and have a new family member for a year.

The great joy in Tajikistan was hiking in the mountains with Gulya. She was an expert mountaineer and knew just how far she could push us on a Sunday hike. The hikes were all day with a rest stop for tea, and we always brought bread, Russian cookies, and hard-boiled eggs. Often there was a swim at the end of the trail in a crystal-clear freezing mountain lake or many river crossings. The altitude made it hard to breathe at first, but the hikes were unforgettable. And driving anywhere in Tajikistan is an adventure in itself. We'd snake along a mountain road in our SUV and look over the edge of the mountain road below and on the particularly bad turns see the rusted hulks of trucks below that didn't make the turn.

Hiking in Tajikistan (or as Bryan's Facebook said Mt. Everest)

One of our officers unfortunately died of a heart attack while jet skiing on a Tajik lake. He was a big man and we had to build his casket. Our legal attaché actually dressed him in a suit so he would look good when he arrived home in the U.S. One of our defense officers accompanied his body and met the family. The dead man had a cell phone with some texts that could have been interpreted as flirting with one of our Tajik employees, or indications of an affair. There was nothing in the regulations to guide us on this one, but to spare the family any more pain I ordered the texts deleted and the phone returned to the family.

STEP 18 – POLISH UP THAT RUSSIAN...
Washington, D.C. 2006–2007

I went back to the Foreign Service Institute and got my "4/4" in Russian, advanced professional proficiency. Now I could work proverbs into my speeches in Russian, something the Russians loved and sometimes only they could figure out. Like:

"его очень трудно найти черного кота в темной квартире, особенно когда его нет! It's very hard to find a black cat in a dark apartment, especially when it's not there!"

Maybe it's a Chinese proverb, but the Russians love it.

...AND GO BACK TO RUSSIA
Vladivostok, Russia 2007–2010

Q: As you are proceeding were you thinking about taking your Russian language skill and remaining in the post-Soviet space or what was your thinking at this point in terms of your career.

ARMBRUSTER: That is funny. It sort of came down to two posts after Dushanbe. Either Barcelona or Vladivostok, Russia. I thought Barcelona would be OK, but I could do some interesting things in Vladivostok. It is such an interesting part of the world where there are still tigers in the wild, the North Korean border and the Russian Arctic. I did the math in my head and thought I would really like to go to Vladivostok. I am glad I did.

One of the most common questions to any Foreign Service Officer is "What do you do all day?"

Well, the American Foreign Service Association recognized the need to answer that question and published *Inside a U.S. Embassy: Diplomacy at Work.* My contribution was from a day in March 2008. You can decide if Barcelona would have been more fun:

6 a.m. I awake on the No. 5 Train. The Okean, which I boarded last night at 7:30 p.m., bound for Khabarovsk from Vladivostok. The birch trees and small settlements that line this stretch of the Trans-Siberian railway come into view. Although this land is still home to some 300 wild tigers and even a few endangered leopards, no wildlife is evident this morning.

6:30 a.m. After my morning "shower" using the sink in the communal bathroom, the train attendant comes by with chai, Russian tea in a glass with a silver holder. The steam fogs the window as we approach Khabarovsk, the second largest city in the Far East. Just a few kilometers from town more factories appear, some obviously from the Soviet days that are in disrepair or abandoned, and some just beginning to bustle. Closer still, there are rail cars on the opposite tracks loaded with huge logs bound for wood-processing factories in China.

8 a.m. My Russian assistant and I arrive in Khabarovsk and we are met by our driver, who drove from Vladivostok the previous day, an eight-hour trip. From the train station we drive to the Parus Hotel on the banks of the Amur River. At the hotel I meet the U.S. Marine attaché who has come from Moscow to participate in our first meeting of the morning.

10 a.m. We arrive at the prison, home for many months to an American citizen charged with murder. As usual, we spend the first 30 minutes showing our documents, making frantic phone calls to higher officials, and eventually convincing the Russian security guards that, yes, we have an appointment, and yes, we will be seeing the American citizen. With that smoothed over, we hand over magazines and food that prison officials will screen and then pass on to the American.

10:30 a.m. We are taken to Investigation Cell One, and the American prisoner is ushered into a booth across from us. He looks good, and as in past visits is informative about prison conditions, interested in news from the outside world, and specific about his few needs and requests. We provide information about the new U.S.-Russian prisoner exchange program and its implications for his case, letting him know that he must decline to appeal his case if he decides to apply for the exchange.

11:30 a.m.

We say goodbye, knowing that we'll be back in a few months but unsure of what he will decide. Ultimately, our job is to inform and provide options. The American prisoner will have to make his own decisions.

12:30 p.m. There are other people involved in the American's case: his lawyers and another U.S. official who has been in Khabarovsk following his case. We meet to compare notes and see if there is anything else we can do to advocate for him.

1 p.m. We have lunch in a typical Russian restaurant where they serve kvass (lightly fermented beer made from black bread), blini, borscht, and caviar, ubiquitous in the Russian Far East.

2:30 p.m. From American citizen services we switch to business development. The Khabarovsk Airport is making a pitch for American freight forwarders to use the Russian airport as a hub for Asian operations. Airport officials argue that costs are lower and logistically that Khabarovsk can serve all of the cities that Seoul can. The case is persuasive, and we promise to provide their briefing to the major document and package companies in the United States.

4 p.m. Our small group walks along the Amur River with Russian environmentalists. The river's water quality has suffered greatly from contamination by Chinese industries and chemical spills, and Russian non-governmental organizations want help improving it. Experts from Portland, Oregon have already provided water monitoring equipment and advice. The river is a beautiful wide waterway that is frozen over now but is obviously a great recreational asset in summer. Even in winter, ice fishermen take advantage of its bounty. Just upriver, we see the museum that will host a poster show we are sponsoring in the spring, a display of U.S. and Soviet war propaganda. We hope that event will allow us to meet some of the surviving World War II heroes.

5 p.m. We arrive at a local university to meet with students who are members of the local USAID-sponsored "Jessup Team." They will attend

*the Jessup International Law Moot World Court competition, with partici-
pants from over 500 law schools in over 80 countries. They will participate
in a mock trial in the United States involving a fictional international law
incident. In this case, a tanker with hazardous materials runs aground
on an island. Who has jurisdiction? Who is liable? For students living in a
city with serious environmental challenges of its own this is a great exercise.
Their rehearsal, in English, is impressive and I wish them well in America.*

*6:30 p.m. We take a quick spin around the city's outdoor ice rink. Kids
and adults of all ages show why Russians win so many figure skating titles.
Some seem more at home on ice than on land. I manage not to fall.*

*8 p.m. We have dinner at the new hockey arena. Unfortunately, there is no
game tonight, but the spaghetti is pretty good in the restaurant overlooking
the rink. The arena is a great new addition to the city. I go over tomorrow's
itinerary: a visit to Komsomolsk-on-Amur where Boeing is working with
the Sukhoi Aircraft Company to build a regional jet that will help make
Vladivostok and Khabarovsk a little less remote. It's one of the best examples
of what the United States and Russia can do when we cooperate, like space
cooperation and our combined efforts in World War II. We'll be up early for
the drive. Who knows, maybe we'll spot a tiger on the way.*

Inside a U.S. Embassy, Diplomacy in Action

Nebraska Publishing

We had another prisoner in our consular district who was housed in Sakhalin.
He was a Korean-American priest and the local authorities wanted the land
where his church was located, so they trumped up charges and arrested him.
The pressure wasn't working and he refused to sell but he was elderly and not
in good health. I sent many démarches to Moscow, asking that they intervene
with foreign ministry officials to no avail. Finally, after months of lobbying,
the Russians said I could go to his parole hearing. I flew to Sakhalin, met with
the man, and then met with the warden. The parole hearing was held in the
prison. The defense lawyer, prosecutor, warden, the inmate, a few guards, and
I took part.

At one point, a guard said to me, "United States! What a country! I can't imagine Russia sending anyone to help me if I were in prison."

He was impressed that the U.S. made the effort on behalf of its citizen. I was told to report to prison the next day for the decision. I got to the parking lot and the pastor was already walking out the gate. His family was there in tears, but he seemed a bit bewildered, as if they might call him back at any second, but I assured him and his family that the decision was final and that he was free. It was a good win. I was coming around to the idea that really the best part of the Foreign Service, was the service.

Q: *Take a moment to describe what Vladivostok is like as a place.*

ARMBRUSTER: It is a port city. We had a lot of great naval ship visits. Culturally it is fantastic. We would bring over jazz artists. We didn't bring Alice Cooper, but he came and did a public diplomacy event with us. We had our 100 best musician and artist contacts over, and he was just the most gracious and terrific host you could imagine.

It is one of the largest consular districts in the world, going from the area across from Alaska all the way down to the North Korean border and then Sakhalin where we had interests as well. It's also a rich area. Rich in oil, rich in forests, rich in seafood. Certainly, in the diversity of the people there, but it is also very sparsely populated. There are some pretty wild areas and the Amur leopard is there.

It is a fascinating part of the world and I have to say we had some of the best locally engaged staff you could imagine. So, for me, diplomatically it was really engaging and interesting. I still think of it as one of my favorite posts, probably because of the people.

Q: *Were you engaged with the Japanese or the Chinese in regional issues?*

ARMBRUSTER: The Japanese certainly. We would compare notes on the political situation. There wasn't the sort of development assistance coordination you might see elsewhere. But certainly I worked with the Japanese. The Chinese Consul General invited me to China to a trade fair, and I rode with him in the car to Northern China. We went to another tiger reserve there. That was quite interesting! I liked my Japanese colleague quite a bit and enjoyed sharing perspectives on economic development.

I also met the North Korean Consul General. Once a year at Christmas they would seat us together and I think we got as far as "Will you pass the salt please?" in terms of our conversation. We never got very far but there was a North Korean restaurant in Vladivostok. Before they did their nuclear test, we did go there. They had pretty good food and very good desserts. But then once the test happened, we just thought that was it.

But you know that small diplomatic presence in Vladivostok is so far removed from Moscow you don't really have that heavy political atmosphere. When relations are bad in Moscow, it is hard to do business. In Vladivostok we were a little bit removed. Even the Russians feel a distance from Moscow and are a little bit freer to do what they want. Caterpillar was very big out there. They sold a lot of equipment. Freightliner, the trucking company, was also very successful in the Russian Far East. It was nice to see some American business ventures moving forward.

Q: Was there any sister city activity with Vladivostok?

ARMBRUSTER: Yes. In fact, flights between Anchorage and Vladivostok were just starting up while I was there, so through the consulate we sponsored a writing contest. We flew the winner, a Russian student, to Anchorage, the sister city. She experienced Alaska for a week and then came back and wrote about it. It was nice to promote those flights. They have been on again, off again. I don't know whether they are on right now. It is close enough that there really should be much deeper links. But you are right, there are some sister city links. San Francisco also has ties to the Russian Far East.

Q: *And your family, were they all with you in Vladivostok?*

ARMBRUSTER: No. by then both our kids were in college, so Kathy did some English teaching in Vladivostok. Our kids did visit. Of course, we would meet them and make a point of getting to wherever we needed to for holidays, but it was just the two of us at that point and our Russian cat Vika. Our dog, Chessie, joined us in Cuba, and traveled to the U.S., Russia, and Mexico. She was a great Foreign Service dog who knew to be nice to GSOs whenever they came into the house unannounced.

Q: *Because of the size of the consular district were there other regional issues within your consular district that kept you busy?*

ARMBRUSTER: We did try to keep a close watch and did some reporting on the North Korean laborers who came across. Every week there was a train. They worked in the timber fields and the seafood industry, and although we visited some places where North Koreans worked, they were always very reluctant to speak to us. We did political reporting. In fact, one of our classified reports on illegal logging made it into *Wikileaks*. We would also report on what Chinese businesses were doing, Chinese tourism and that kind of thing, as well as American.

Q: *Did your consular district go all the way up to the Arctic? Were there any Arctic issues you had to deal with?*

ARMBRUSTER: It did go up to the Arctic to Chukotka which is a stunning place, but the links between U.S. and Russian communities were not very deep. Indigenous people travel back and forth, depending on how warm the relations are. But it didn't take up much of our diplomatic energy. We went to the regions once a quarter to see what was going on and look at the investments.

A lot of Vladivostok was devoted to the military. For example, the *Blue Ridge*, flagship of our Pacific Fleet, came to visit and the admiral invited me to go back with him onboard to Japan and give a lecture to the sailors about the Foreign Service and the State Department and what a consulate is. That was a real highlight. The sailors were just great diplomats. They came and played volleyball and basketball and were out on the streets in their uniforms. They just do a great job representing America.

Q: *What about environmental issues?*

ARMBRUSTER: There definitely were environmental issues. In fact, we even heard rumors of long-ago radioactive release that had contaminated the area and actually caused the deaths of some people way back during the depths of the Cold War when that type of thing was absolutely secret. I guess it still is. But we would hear things like that from the locals. You couldn't really swim in the local area and Exxon was working on Sakhalin, so they were always trying to make sure they had good relations with the locals and did things right so they didn't go afoul of the environmental regulations. Of course, deforestation is an issue and the environment in general, because it is such a rich area, was always on our minds.

Q: *So, from here were there any career lessons for whatever you were going to next?*

ARMBRUSTER: I think I learned the depth and the strength of the locally engaged staff (LES).

They were often the movers and shakers, especially on the musical guests that would come. We also had a visit from coach Tom Newell, a former NBA coach, who conducted basketball clinics throughout the Russian Far East. He was a tremendous hit. He would not only cover the X's and O's of basketball, but he would give whatever message you needed, "stay in school, stay off drugs…", just a real great guy. He was again one of those ambassadors of the United States that was great to have. The locally engaged staff knew just where to take him and how to best use him and present him to the Russian audience. I can't say enough about the Russian LES in Vladivostok.

———————

I did see Siberian tigers. Not the way Kostya, my driver, did, alone and in the forest. But one on a slab unfortunately for an autopsy. The others in a home-made very Russian preserve. An elderly man and his wife ran the operation and relied on donations. The tigers had a fairly large area to play in and they were obviously loved by the man. He was dead set against radio collars, saying they interfered with the animals own navigational system and he thought that was why so many were killed on the roads. He had foxes and other animals as well. On a trip to Northern China I saw a state-run tiger preserve and saw a live goat released into the pen and immediately eaten. Vladivostok is famous in Russia for its "Tiger Day" celebration when the kids dress as tigers and conservation groups get their messages out.

My hope in Vladivostok was that the contentious Moscow-Washington relationship would be a little less tense in the Far East. I knew that the Peace Corps volunteers who had served in the Russian Far East were still regarded by Russians as friends. They remembered them by name, and they served America well, until Putin decided they were spies and pretty much anything American was suspect.

So, I tried to advance people-to-people diplomacy in any way I could. We sponsored a writing contest and the winner went on one of the first flights from Vladivostok to Anchorage. She was a young college student and had a great time. But, as always it was one step forward, two steps back. Those flights were eventually discontinued; again, for political reasons.

I also noticed that a black, classic train steam engine was on display on the railway platform. Upon closer inspection, I saw it was made in Minnesota or someplace. After a little more research we discovered it was one of the lend-lease trains from World War II. I commissioned a plaque and a visiting Navy captain joined me in the plaque ceremony.

There were other wins as well. Alice Cooper for one. When we heard he was coming to play Vlad we got in touch with the manager and asked if he would be interested in meeting with Russian musicians and artists. He said yes. We organized a barbeque at one of the consulate townhouses, invited 100 of our best Russian contacts from the arts community and had a blast. Alice was gracious, listening to teens bang out their hits and chatting with everyone. I went to the concert later and was invited backstage, but the Russians had been so difficult about access for me I decided to just be happy I got in the door and didn't try to get backstage. I've always wished I'd gone for it, but hey, I was worthy.[18]

Me and Alice Cooper – just hangin'

The most long-lasting public diplomacy event was with NBA coach, Tom Newell. Tom is a force of nature. An eternal spring of good vibes, positive messages for kids, and great fundamental basketball. I saw him coaching a Chinese team that came to play against the Vladivostok Spartak team. I chatted him up and asked if he could come back for a program for kids. He could. On the first visit we sent him to Blagoveshchensk on the train with a Russian

---

18   Reference to Cooper's catch phrase from Wayne's World. https://www.nme.com/news/music/alice-cooper-reflects-legendary-waynes-world-scene-25-years-later-1970567

public diplomacy staffer. Tom has never let me forget that I put him on that overnight train. And now that I think about it, putting an American coach on a Russian train headed to a Russian border town just across from China, with no Russian language training, was kind of a big ask!

I went with him on the next trip upcountry in the Far East. The first game we played against each other and I played hard. I was winded and about to die. Finally, I was taking off on a fast break and he grabbed the back of my T-shirt. "Hey, man! Slow down, we're just having fun!" Whew! I'm glad he said that!

I would help Tom coach, bringing in embassy messages about fitness, staying off drugs, and staying in school. Later, Tom came to the Marshall Islands and he has had a tremendous impact around the world.

Kathy was the star of another public diplomacy triumph. We'd had some success with culinary diplomacy, pitting U.S. Navy chefs against local chefs. So, a local TV station decided to invite us on their show to cook our signature pizzas. We had been making pizza since Cuba, when we would invite one of the Marines over for dinner every Friday. The show went well, entirely in Russian, until the time we opened our homemade ginger ale. Under the hot TV lights the already fermented ginger ale was ready to explode. Sure enough, once the Russian host twisted the cap the ginger ale exploded all over the studio. They took it well though, and the pizza was great, so we escaped the Gulag.

But above rock stars and NBA coaches there is one celebrity that beats them all. Astronauts. We had a photo exhibit and movies showing with an astronaut and cosmonaut. Kathy danced with the cosmonaut which she *never* stops talking about, and everybody loved the astronaut. During a tour of NASA's photo exhibit of the moon landing the cosmonaut stopped in his tracks at the photo of the footprint on the moon. He silently wiped away a tear and moved on.

The travel in the Russian Far East was terrific. Sakhalin, Kamchatka, Chukotka. The places sound remote and exotic and they are. I was able to swim in the sea in Sakhalin. Soak in a natural hot spring in Kamchatka, and visit the Chukotka, the northernmost part of our consular district. There you would see outdoor markets operating full steam in minus 40-degree weather. Vats of caviar and frozen fish lined the market. It was like a scene from a Star Wars bar. But in town, we found bowling alleys and pizza places and other modern trappings in a land that was once reserved for reindeer herders.

Before I arrived in Vladivostok one of my predecessors was involved in an accident in which a Russian was badly injured and paralyzed. He was not compensated, with the U.S. claiming sovereign immunity. The Russian man often protested, and I felt it was a distraction, and more than that it was just wrong. The U.S. driver had also claimed diplomatic immunity, and right or wrong, I knew that there would have been insurance money for the man if the driver was not a diplomat.

Of course diplomats do have immunity and claim it with varying degrees of effectiveness. In Finland a drunk ambassador was pulled over by the police and told to get out of the car. He refused. They urged him to call a driver. He refused. They said they would drive him home. No. He was going to drive himself. Diplomatic immunity. The policeman nodded his head. OK. He stepped away from the car. A shot rang out. Then another. And another. And one more. The policeman returned to the driver side. "You can drive home now." Of course he had shot out all four tires. Diplomacy is all about figuring out the next move. You lost that round, ambassador.

I drove several hours away to a nondescript apartment building and met with "Sergei," the accident victim. He invited me, wheeled himself into the living room and we chatted. He said he wanted enough money for an operation and a chance to walk again. I said I'd try. He was still angry, bitter, but we were negotiating, and I felt hopeful.

So I went to work on Washington, arguing that a visit by the ambassador to the Far East would be overshadowed by this case when we should be promoting trade links with the U.S. West Coast.

Meanwhile, the man had gone on a hunger strike. The embassy sent me talking points for the press. I got a call from the Deputy Chief of Mission after hours,

Moscow being a day in time zones away. The DCM was adamant that we hold the press release and work quietly with Sergei to arrange a deal. I hesitated. I knew that I had given the release to my press officer, but it being late, I didn't know if he had given it to the press yet. And I worried that if Sergei died from the hunger strike the U.S. would get the blame. I knew we were making a good faith effort and didn't want this to be another reason for the Russians to argue the Americans were to blame for every bad thing in Russia.

The next day I gave a speech at the local university, was done by 10 a.m. and flew to Niigata, Japan for a few days off to ski. I flew into Niigata Airport a couple hours after takeoff, got through customs in no time, hopped on a bus, then a train, then got picked up by the hotel, and soon found myself skiing in beautiful Japan. It was a perfect day. The next morning started with a great, healthy Japanese breakfast. I smiled and realized I had not smiled in a long time. I relaxed. And then the phone rang.

The DCM was on the phone. Everything had fallen apart with Sergei and he wanted to let me know the ambassador was not happy with me and that I had not been straight with him by not telling him the press release might have already gone from the consulate. Guilty. I felt terrible. And more punishment for this good deed was coming. But not for a while. In the end, Sergei did get his compensation, but not until the next consul general arrived. Washington had pushed the case and $50,000 came through.

A new ambassador arrived in Moscow and made the trip to Vladivostok. He got off the plane in a black mood. He barely spoke to us on the way to the first event, a wild leopard reserve right on the North Korean border. And then we got there. Being out in nature and seeing the good work we were doing with our Russian partners immediately brightened the ambassador's mood. We did all kinds of events with the ambassador, most of them outside. He met with youth in Khabarovsk at the university, he took in the arts and culture of Vladivostok, and he left very happy.

The Russian staff at the consulate were some of the best local staff I'd ever worked with. Kostya, my driver, was a rock. We'd drive all day on ice roads and through forests and he never faltered, got sleepy, or failed to chat when I wanted to, or find a place in those long empty stretches for us to get something to eat, often squid for some reason. He was great. And Lena, my secretary, set up every meeting knowing that I liked a packed schedule and figuring out our trips to the second.

And then there were Zhenya and Dima. Both in the public diplomacy section and both super talented. Every jazz musician who came to Vlad was taken care of by Zhenya and most are still friends with her. The public diplomacy unit also had the audacity to invite the Long Island Youth Orchestra to the Far East with a multi-city itinerary. And they had to find host families to take care of the dozens of kids along with their moms and dads who made the trip. They pulled it off, like they pulled off so many other great events. For example, Zhenya somehow came up with a white mustache and white beard and I found myself in front of a packed university hall in full Mark Twain regalia, giving a speech as Mark Twain himself. We even had enough handy quotes like: "Go to heaven for the climate, hell for the company" and "Patriotism is supporting your country all the time, and your government when it deserves it." I was able to take questions from the crowd and stay in character, knowing a lot of those quotes were all purpose. It was tremendous fun. I figured a slow, midwestern accent would do the trick.

Engaging with Russian students was always fun. We debated politics. I asked them about the world. One room full of people did not know who Tiger Woods was, at the top of his fame. One student said, "A basketball player? He's some kind of sports person." It was a good reminder that the world doesn't always see America as we do and is not especially consumed by our superstars. The only student request I turned down was a request to sing. I just didn't think I would represent America well on that.

Travel is, of course, the great perk of the Foreign Service. To go to Kamchatka and Sakhalin and Chukotka in the Far North is a pure pleasure. Chukhotka could be minus 40 in winter. Their motto is "The Land of Real People." You have to be real to survive those kinds of temperatures; real adept at keeping warm, keeping close friends when you need them, and real good at hunting or fishing if you don't have a steady job.

On a train trip to Khabarovsk the new DCM Eric Rubin and I discussed Stalin and Russia's history. It was a great trip and nice to share thoughts on the – sometimes inscrutable – Russians. Eric also started one sentence with "When you are ambassador..." It floored me, since I never really thought I would achieve that rank. I thought it might be nice to be DCM once, but ambassador? Are you kidding me! It was nice to hear and got me thinking a little bit....

Zhenya was one of the most talented Russians on our staff. Her real love was music and she took care of dozens of jazz and classical musicians, introducing them to the Russian Far East and delighting discerning Russian listeners with something new every time. I loved all of the Russian consulate staffers and they are part of the reason I still have hope for Russia. Russians are so cultured, so smart, and not served well by their current system. But history is history. They have come a long way and have a long way to go.

Another patron of the arts, and an artist herself, was Larisa Belobrova, the governor's wife. A talented and beautiful movie star, she and Kathy hit it off. On Veterans Day they knocked back vodka shots and smoked old school cigarettes. When Kathy left Vlad and was on her way to the airport, she saw a black limo speeding beside her. It turned out to be Larisa. They had always joked about getting tattoos together, so stick on tattoos were produced and they drank some more and got tattooed in the VIP lounge. Soft power diplomacy!

When I first arrived, Governor Darkin invited me on to his yacht for his daughter's birthday. I was hesitant. I didn't know how close I wanted to get to a Russian politician/businessman. I expressed my misgivings on the phone to a colleague at the embassy in Moscow. The next day the invitation was withdrawn. But Kathy and Larissa Belobrova's friendship never wavered. Kathy, the wife of a man most Russians would consider a spy, and Larissa, the wife of a man most Americans would see as a mobster. But two very charming women trying – and succeeding – to make their way.

Kathy's other great friend was Tai-san, the wife of the Japanese cultural officer. They were our tennis buddies on Sundays. They probably won 60 percent of the time, but we came through every now and then. The remarkable thing is that our common language was Russian as they didn't speak English and we didn't speak Japanese, and to this day Kathy and Tae have a weekly chat in Russian on Skype. Kathy's Russian now is probably better than mine.

◆

In Arsenyiev there is a softball field, probably the only one around for thousands of square miles, and the local team invited us to play. We teed off on the ball. I was lucky enough to have Bryan in town and he started off with a home run. We never looked back and beat the local team, as any self-respecting American consulate would. I even got into a mock Earl Weaver vs Umpire showdown,[19] complete with throwing dirt on the home plate and throwing my cap on the ground. The crowd was a little unsure of whether it was theater or not, but we had a great time. A few weeks later we got a photo album. I felt a little like Keira Knightley in *Love Actually* when she sees the video of her wedding. "The pictures... they're all... of me." The mayor's cameraman must have been instructed to take shots of the American Consul General, 'cause all of those pictures were of me!

A real American rock star in Vladivostok and all of Russia really is Rock Brynner, son of movie star Yul Brynner. Rock was invited to Vlad many years ago to attend the Pacific Meridian International Film Festival. As luck would have it, Rock's family practically founded Vladivostok. The Brynners finally fled the communists through China and made their way to the U.S. via Switzerland. Yul's heritage was always something of a mystery in Hollywood, so he could play anyone, from cowboy to King of Siam.

Rock's life was no less colorful than his dad's. He was Mohammed Ali's bodyguard for a time, he married one of Charlie's Angels, he was in with the biggest rockers of the day and is friends with James Earl Jones. He is bigger than life, but Vladivostok and Russia touched Rock deeply. Rediscovering the roots of his family and representing the family's legacy there was profound.

---

[19]   Earl Weaver was a diminutive coach for the Baltimore Orioles baseball team in the 1960s and 70s and was famous for his temper tantrums with umpires.

His book *Empire and Odyssey* details some of the Brynner accomplishments in commerce in the Far East and a wonderful statue of his dad stands in Vladivostok outside of the family's home.

I enjoyed meeting Rock, and he was engaging with everyone. He gave a great lecture at Vladivostok University on the history of rock 'n' roll and the intersection of rock with the civil rights movement. Russian students loved it. His life is so much richer for taking the chance on that first trip when he really didn't know anyone. And the culture of the Far East is enriched by Rock's continued presence at the festival every year. One year he even brought his friend Liza Minnelli. Hard to imagine they could walk anywhere without the paparazzi showing up!

The other VIP visits were American ships to the port of Vladivostok: "breasting barges,"

"Yokahama fenders," and "Med moorings." These are just some of the naval terms staff of the

U.S. Consulate General in Vladivostok have become familiar with as they facilitate "ship visits" – the arrival of a U.S. Navy destroyer, cutter, or minesweeper. The visits have led to chess matches between sailors and local children, and to cook-offs, jazz concerts, and volleyball games for naval personnel. There have also been talks between high-level personnel of the U.S. and Russian navies and participation in marches to mark the U.S./Russian joint victory in World War II.

Some of the Navy ships the post has greeted include the USS *Blue Ridge*, USS *Cowpens*, and USS *Stethem*. As Consul General, I enjoyed seeing sailors on the city's streets interacting with local Russians, and seeing a ship come through the fog flying the Stars and Stripes, is a tremendous morale boost at a remote post like Vladivostok.

On departure, ships often played *Stars and Stripes Forever* on their loudspeakers, another patriotic pleasure.

Dozens of ship visits have occurred at Pier 33 in Vladivostok, the city that is headquarters for the Russian Pacific Fleet. In May, the USS *Blue Ridge* arrived with a crew of 1,200 sailors and Marines who had arrived to help Russia celebrate the 65th anniversary of the end of WWII. They docked alongside Russian warships. As with other visits, the city's leaders welcomed the navy's goodwill ambassadors with handshakes and a traditional ceremony involving bread and the sprinkling of salt.

Commander Paul Lyons of the *USS* Stethem partakes of the traditional Russian bread and salt welcome

U.S.-Russian military meetings such as ship visits are often planned a year in advance. However, schedules for the ship visit itself may not be fully developed until about three weeks prior to the ship's arrival. Due to the consulate's size, these meetings require the help of all personnel. The consulate seeks out the special interest of the ship's personnel too, since American sailors are often eager for sports competitions, even exotic ones such as dragon boat races. The post organizes outreach efforts such as visits to orphanages, children's cancer wards, and veterans' centers, and plans time buy the paint and supplies that visitors can use to spruce up some of these facilities. The visit of the USS *Blue Ridge*, for instance, required the consulate to coordinate more than 15 events.

The consulate also works with the local authorities to arrange protocol meetings between the ship's commanders and the city's mayor and other officials.

Post FSNs are as much a part of the visit as the Americans. My secretary, Lena Vasilevskaya – nicknamed "Admiral Lena" – coordinated many of the community relations events. She loved to see soccer matches and basketball games involving U.S. and Russian sailors and, like the rest of us, had a soft spot for seeing Russian youngsters defeat American sailors at chess. (Tip: Don't play against Russians in hockey or chess if you want to win.)

Generally speaking, ship visits are treated like the visits of any other high-level visitor. Commanders are provided a briefing on the current economic and political situation and then the post arranges welcome and security briefings on the ship or at the consulate. When possible, I would go out to the arriving navy ship with the Russian pilot boat to welcome the navy captain. On shore, our American staff met with navy counterparts in the consulate and answered questions about everything, from economics in the region and Vladivostok's preparations for the Asia Pacific Economic Cooperation Forum (APEC) in 2012, to the best nightclubs.

The post also worked with Russia's naval attaché to ensure that the senior U.S. Navy officer gets the meetings needed with his or her Russian counterparts. *Security issues are worked out with a navy advance team that determines limits for sailors' shore leave, or liberty.* (Most are due back on board at midnight known as "Cinderella Liberty.")

Vice Admiral John M. Bird said that Vladivostok is a favorite port for American sailors. Once a closed city, off limits even to Russians during the Cold War, Bird says part of the fascination for veteran sailors is that they never imagined visiting Russia when they joined the Navy, some as much as 20 or so years ago. Younger sailors, of course, enjoy the nightlife, and few sailors of any age like having to be back by midnight.

During ship visits, the Russian press has a field day, often seeking unusual photos such as that of the Russian boy with his hands on the ship's wheel on the bridge, or in the ship's command center. Consulate Press expert, Dmitriy Motovilov said he was overwhelmed with press requests when a ship arrived with a female Navy captain. Russian women were openly emotional seeing Captain Holly Graf in command and were impressed by her professionalism and poise. There are no female Russian Navy captains – or even female sailors. According to RusNavy.com women only serve in support roles on shore.

As Russia considers professionalizing its Navy to a greater extent, it need look no further than the U.S. Navy model – at least as we've seen it during ship visits – and American sailors take away great memories too. Commander Paul Lyons of USS *Stethem* has a picture hanging in his living room of the port of Vladivostok. "Fond memories," he says, "of a great visit."

The flagship of the U.S. Pacific Fleet also visited Vladivostok – USS *Blue Ridge*. The admiral invited me aboard to talk to sailors about the Foreign Service. I hitched a ride with the ship from Vladivostok to Yokohama and had quite a suite near the captain's quarters. Needless to say I was in heaven. I also found time to go out on deck and feel at once the power of the ship and the vastness of the ocean.

There is a postscript to ship visits. For years in the Pacific "Fat Leonard" had been corrupting naval officers, treating them to wine, women, and song in local karaoke bars in exchange for intel on the ship's movements. With that info, he could get a jump on contracts for provisioning the ships with food, water, and fuel. Several navy officers have gone to jail and at least one committed suicide. My friend, Captain Lyons was one of the targets of Fat Leonard and his deputy had been in on it. Captain Lyons' faith, family, and values were rock solid. He was "dinged" by association but had a terrific naval career and is one of many great Americans I had the pleasure to meet during my career.

Bryan and Kalia both visited us in Vladivostok. Bryan took the trans-Siberian from Vladivostok to Moscow, then St Petersburg, and on to Helsinki. The trip of a lifetime. The trip also involved an adventure with him hanging on to the train after a mix-up at a stop. Bryan was left hanging on outside the train with his girlfriend running along on the tracks behind the train. As a dad, I didn't want to know more details. I was just glad they were both safe.

So, future ambassador, I'm going to tell you that you will make missteps in your career, but I did you the favor of doing the dumbest thing a diplomat could do. Diplomatic dinners and receptions are part of our trade. It's the stereotype of diplomatic life, but they also serve a function; information gets traded and a less formal atmosphere lets you gauge a little better what your diplomatic colleagues are up to and why. We were invited to the Japanese Consul General's residence. Just a small group of us. As we settled into the living room for drinks before a dinner of sushi imported from Japan, there was one of those uncomfortable silences. Being the skilled diplomat that I am, I looked around the room for something to comment on. Kathy caught my eye just as I settled on a photograph and she raised her index finger, which being a skilled husband, I also knew meant 'No. Don't do it, don't say it. For God's sake, don't go there!' But, being the skilled diplomat, I blundered on… I smiled and said, "Are those your parents?" I could see Kathy bury her face in her hands. The Consul General drew himself up to full attention, "No. That is the emperor and empress of Japan." Yeah. Thanks. I knew that.

Saying goodbye in Vlad took place at the consulate townhouses. There was a long driveway. Kostya let me off at the top of it and asked me to wait. Then a bunch of guys came up the driveway with a kayak. They told me to get in. I did, and they carried me down to the farewell party. At the end, I asked everybody to line up. I gave everyone a high five and said, "Good game, good game, good game…" I was crying by the end.

The bidding came down to Vietnam and another consul general job or New York as a recruiter for State as Diplomat in Residence. With our daughter in NYC, and having been away for three years, I didn't let the game play out and took the New York job, even though it was less prestigious and "promotable." Sometimes family trumps everything. Sometimes family rolls with the next thing.

STEP 19 – BECOME A DIPLOMAT IN RESIDENCE
New York City 2010–2012

Kathy often thought that her career was just a patchwork quilt of gigs here or there, not really amounting to a body of work. Well, don't they say something about New York that if you can make it here, you can make it anywhere? *New York, New York?* Kathy's resume and global experience landed her a librarian job on the Upper West Side in about five minutes. I think she submitted the resume on Friday and was scheduling the interview on Monday, and the school had been looking for a long time. All of her experience overseas paid off and it was great to see Kathy where she belongs, with lots of kids and lots of books. And I could literally see her from our apartment; we had found a place on Columbus Avenue and 100th Avenue on the Upper West Side and Kathy worked across the street, on about the same floor.

My job was further uptown at the City College of New York in Harlem. Colin Powell's school. I recruited in New York, New Jersey, Connecticut, and Pennsylvania. It sounds like a lot of territory but with the trains, planes, and rental cars at my disposal I got to hundreds of venues and talked to students, veterans, anybody interested in the Foreign Service. I also taught "Understanding Russia" and "The Practice of Diplomacy" at City College.

I met Colin Powell when he came to the City College, NY. He had his book, so I got my signed copy and I gave him a copy of *Inside a U.S. Embassy* with my Vladivostok story.

Colin Powell was a great leader of the troops at State. Inspirational, interested in the institution, and a forceful advocate for the U.S. Maybe too forceful at the UN. His defense of the Iraq War and chemical weapons did him in politically, but there hasn't been as talented a Republican being talked about for president since Powell.

Colin Powell paging through *Inside a US Embassy*

Somewhere I have an exchange between Colin Powell and I: I wrote to him urging him to run for president. I envisioned an ad campaign. It starts with a road and Colin Powell saying "Some people say I am too middle of the road. I don't think so." (Camera accelerates with the road) "I think America is ready to move forward (shot of the centerline speeds up, reveals it is a runway, jet takes off) and we're ready to fly."

Something like that. I told him I was a Foreign Service Officer, that was maybe my third tour, well before Iraq and Afghanistan. He wrote back saying maybe I should consider switching careers, from diplomacy to politics. Nice letter. I still have it somewhere.

Q: That is fantastic.

ARMBRUSTER: At that time, we had priority internships – paid internships – for a select number of minority students. They choose six really talented people. I know at least one has entered the Foreign Service. It was really great to recruit, especially second-generation Americans who were very bright, very talented, and looking to change the world. I enjoyed recruiting and seeing their eyes light up as they think 'this is something I can do!' The only difficulty for the second-generation Americans was the diplomatic security background check took longer for them because they not only had to check their U.S. contacts, but also their contacts from their country of origin. Sometimes that would take so long, they would drop out of the process. I wish they could come up with a system where it is 100 days for everybody, it doesn't matter where you are from. Because these are definitely people who want to serve and have something to contribute.

Q: *And often they spoke other languages.*

ARMBRUSTER: They did. We had one student from the University of Pennsylvania who spoke Albanian, did an internship in Albania, and is now serving as an FSO.

Q: *What were the surprises for you, I mean coming back to the U.S. after all this time and interacting with the students, especially after you had gone to school and done some academic work. What were the surprises and the takeaways during this time you were interacting with students?*

ARMBRUSTER: The biggest shock for me – and it was a really pleasant one – is that they really got it. They understood that it was expeditionary diplomacy now. That you were going to Afghanistan and Iraq and working in the provisional reconstruction teams and supporting the military. Earlier on there was such a stereotype about the Foreign Service that we are cookie pushers and it is all cocktail parties and that kind of thing. These kids had done their research about the real work of embassies that they knew it was prison visits and working on the visa lines. I don't think they had the illusions that earlier generations did about diplomatic life. For them it wasn't necessarily glamorous. It was service. I just found them to be very talented and ready to go and contribute.

One of the problems with the Foreign Service profession is that you move a lot! And things get lost. The only treasure I really miss is a picture that Kalia drew when she was four of a girl dancing in the rain with a rainbow. Maybe it will turn up someday. Oh, and the Gene Roddenberry interview. I interviewed the Star Trek creator in Waikiki. We had a nice half-hour long chat and I put it all on a reel to reel tape and kept it. Hawaii Public Radio probably aired a three-minute segment from that. *Somewhere,* I have the whole interview and would love to find it for his fans, including me!

One of the things I did while recruiting students was a simulation I called "Game Day." I would break the class into three teams, the host country, the White House, and the

embassy. Then I'd have them plan a Presidential visit. As they planned, I'd throw in curveballs, making the visit just one day instead of three, throwing in a crisis in the region, or the arrest of an American. Here is what each team received:

Game Day

White House Team

Your Secret Objectives for the Presidential Visit:
Start a serious relationship with the Host Government and attempt to grapple with longstanding bilateral problems.
Show the world we are not anti-Islam.
No museums.
Have at least one "deliverable," e.g., an environmental or scientific agreement.
Avoid photo ops with the "Maximum Jefe" that are too informal or "fun."
Show folks back home that the administration is working to spread democracy.
Show that the president is tough on tyrants like the Maximum Jefe.

Host Country

Your Secret Objectives for the Visit:

Show the world that you belong on the world stage.

Have the president visit the national museum since the First Brother or Sister runs it.
Relatively low domestic profile due to rampant anti-Americanism.
No open press or public fora where unscripted questions could be asked.
Show off Host Country culture and natural treasures.
No big negotiations.
Security a top priority.

Embassy Team

Objectives:

"Successful" visit, good domestic, and international press.
Build new relationships with Host Country.
Begin student exchange program, funded by Congress but blocked by Host Government.
A presidential visit with embassy families.
Embassy briefing for the president.
Visit to USAID project.
Visit to the International School attended by Americans and Host Country (elite) children.

It played out differently every time, but the trick was that the president's "no museums" maxim was just an offhand comment he made after touring a museum in Bucharest for three hours. In the game, if really pressed, the president would agree to a short tour. But presidential visits are dynamic and fluid, and the game reflects that.

Another game I like to play is the perfect day... Imagining a perfect day if travel were instantaneous. It might start with breakfast in the Marshall Islands, with breadfruit and eggs – a nice combo – a fresh coconut, and coffee. Then, a morning swim in Honolulu at Sans Souci beach, swimming out to the orange flag, saying hello to the local turtle and heading back. From there, a walk-through of Central Park in New York City, then lunch in Helsinki and some skiing in Japan. From there, maybe a show in Moscow and dinner in Mexico City.

There are a few givens in the Foreign Service: 1) you have to be available world-wide, you can't just do countries with palm trees; and 2) you have to enunciate U.S. policy. At a Yale event I admitted that sometimes when a friend overseas asked about a U.S. policy that I disagreed with I would explain it this way: "There is a wide spectrum of opinion in the U.S. The administration's position is here, the left's position is here, and the right's position is here, and personally, I'm right about here." A former ambassador came up to me after the event and said, "I don't agree with you. As ambassador you have to enunciate the administration policy period. Your own views don't count overseas." I think he's right. In an authoritarian country, where the press is limited, it's good to show the diversity of opinion in the U.S. and the ongoing robust debate, but ambassadors do get paid big bucks to advocate for the policy and the administration in power. I stood corrected. Although we have our own opinions, we have to "talk the talk" overseas, or resign.

As I said in the interview, I learned on my recruiting trips that this generation "gets it" to a greater degree than older people. They know the Foreign Service consists of hardship tours and unaccompanied tours away from your family. They understand there are multiple career tracks, with political, economic, consular and management offices, and they want to serve. What they are not sure of is whether the State Department wants them and they are often hesitant to take the test.

I always say take it! The State Department doesn't average your scores, they don't care how many times you take it, and the record is someone who took it something like 13 times and finally got in. I hope she loves it. I took it three or four times too. It's a fun test. It takes a few hours out of your life, then you can go back to whatever you are doing. Besides, the security background investigation takes months. And it is even longer if you have extensive overseas experience or foreign ties, which I think is discriminatory. There should be a standard clock for each applicant, a yea or nay in six months for example. That would be fair.

Bidding from New York City I bid on positions in Kabul but did not get a nibble from the bureau. I also sent out some longshot bids for Chief of Mission jobs. I have the letter I sent for the job in Micronesia. Each bureau asks for a Chief of Mission statement. Here's mine for Micronesia:

MICRONESIA – Inter-agency, Isolation, Econ Development, Regional Experience

On the U.S.-Mexican border I co-led the Border Liaison Mechanism with my Mexican counterpart and we involved dozens of local, state, and federal officials in our border security efforts. I took that experience to Tajikistan where I formed a Border Law Enforcement Working Group to coordinate efforts between the military and civilian agencies, as well as NGOs and the United Nations. I've supervised USAID, Agriculture, and worked with the military many times.

When I joined, it was more about the adventure – kayaking from Helsinki to Tallinn, testing a survival suit off the deck of a nuclear icebreaker, and cross-country cycling around Cuba. Now, it is the service that stays with me. For example, leading a business delegation from Tajikistan to Kunduz, Afghanistan to promote regional development, coordinating a humanitarian relief effort in Magadan, Russia, and securing the release of an American pastor from an unjust imprisonment are a few of the examples.

American interests are global and it's a world in transition. On the Tajik-Afghan border, in Iqaluit, Canada and in Cuban prisons, all remote places to be sure, I've advanced American diplomacy. I've also been a nuclear affairs officer, lead negotiator for a treaty, and control officer for numerous presidential, Secretary of State, and Congressional delegations. Whether at the center of the action in a high profile visit, or thousands of miles from the embassy aboard the USS Blue Ridge, it all matters. From the local guard to the ambassador, everyone contributes, and as a leader I try to instill a sense of pride and mission in everything we do.

In Vladivostok I became aware of the importance of the Asia-Pacific Economic Cooperation forum and traveled with a delegation to China for a meeting in the run-up to Russia's hosting of the 2012 APEC meeting.

Micronesia plays its part in the global community and U.S. interests range from economic development, to fishing rights, to climate change. Knowing that it is a world in transition, with the U.S. also evolving and changing, the privilege of serving as Chief of Mission brings the best opportunity to make sense of and lead change in a positive direction for both countries. As Charge, DCM, and Consul General in Central Asia, the Western Hemisphere, and Europe, I understand America's global reach, promise and goals.

I joined the Foreign Service from Hawaii and serving in the Pacific would be coming full circle.

Level of Interest: High

MARSHALL ISLANDS – Isolation, Inter-agency, Political/Military, Negotiating, Economic

Development/Reform

I imagine the one to the Marshall Islands was quite similar. I was asked which I would choose if I had a choice. I said the Marshall Islands due to the nuclear legacy, military base, and complexity of the relationship. I think I chose well.

My other sideline in New York was volunteering to be an auxiliary New York Police Officer. I took the training, never used it, and as an auxiliary we never carried weapons. My beat was on Broadway from about 90th street to 110th. Most often we just gave directions to the subway. And every night we took a break and talked about where we would go. We'd talk about the Turkish place, the Japanese place, the German deli. But every night, someone would say, 'I know! Let's go to Hot and Crusty's!' And sure enough, every time that's where we went for a slice of pizza and a coke.

STEP 20 – GET CONFIRMED
Washington, D.C. 2012

At the Senate confirmation hearing I was joined by several other nominees. We sat in a row, gave our remarks, and answered the Senators' questions. During one answer, a fellow nominee leaned over and whispered in my ear, "If confirmed." I guess I dropped that, but as you'll see in the testimony, I said it *ten* times in the remarks! But there is the story of one Ambassador-designate who never made it to post because a Senator overheard him say he was "going to be the next ambassador to Country X." It didn't work out that way in confirmation.

Testimony of Thomas Armbruster Ambassador-Designate to the Republic of the Marshall Islands Statement Before the Senate Foreign Relations Committee July 18, 2012

Madam Chairman, Ranking Member Barrasso, Members of the Committee, it is an honor to appear before you today as President Obama's nominee to be the U.S. Ambassador to the Republic of the Marshall Islands (RMI). I am thankful to President Obama and Secretary Clinton for the confidence shown in me by this nomination. If confirmed, I would welcome the chance to work with you, this Committee, and other Members of Congress to advance American interests in the Pacific.

I would like to introduce my wife Kathy and son Bryan who, along with our daughter Kalia, have traveled every step of my career path from Hawaii to Finland to Cuba, Russia, Mexico, Tajikistan, and New York serving the United States in the Foreign Service.

The Marshall Islands is a key partner in the United States' deepening commitment to the Pacific. Secretary Clinton said: 'One of the most important tasks of American statecraft over the next decade will be to lock in a substantially increased investment – diplomatic, economic, strategic, and otherwise – in the Asia-Pacific region.' The United States and the Marshall Islands have a close and special relationship dating back to the end of the Second World War, when the Marshall Islands became part of the UN Trust Territory of the Pacific Islands under the administration of the United

States. In 1986, the Marshall Islands and the United States signed the Compact of Free Association and the RMI became an independent state.

This Compact, which was amended in 2004 to extend economic assistance for an additional 20 years, provides the framework for much of our bilateral relationship. Under the Compact, citizens of the RMI can live, study, and work in the United States without a visa. The Compact obliges the two countries to consult on matters of foreign policy, and the RMI government has an excellent voting affinity with the United States in the United Nations, sharing our positions on many contentious issues, including human rights and Israel. Mutual security of our nations is an underlying element of the special relationship between the United States and the Republic of Marshall Islands. Under the Compact the United States has committed to defend the Marshall Islands as if it were part of our own territory, as the RMI has no military of its own.

Marshallese citizens serve in our armed forces, volunteering at a higher rate than citizens from any individual state. Jefferson Bobo was the first Marshallese cadet to graduate from the Coast Guard Academy in May 2011. He will do his part to defend global peace and security, in peacekeeping missions, in U.S.-led combat operations, and in patrolling the world's waterways. If confirmed, I will work closely with the host government and the Marshallese people to ensure such mutual benefits of our close relationship are widely recognized.

The United States also enjoys complete access to Marshallese ports, airports, and airspace, a vital asset for our defense and security needs. The Marshall Islands hosts the U.S. Army's Ronald Reagan Ballistic Missile Defense Test Site on Kwajalein (known as USAKA). The base is the country's second largest employer, second only to government services. I met with General Formica and his talented and dedicated team at the Space and Missile Defense Command Headquarters in Huntsville and know how important their work is. The test site plays a significant role in the U.S. missile defense research, development, and testing network. It is used to monitor foreign launches and provide deep-space tracking and is an ideal near-equator launch site for satellites. Under the Amended Compact, the United States has access to Kwajalein through 2066 with the option to extend until 2086. Continued access is important, but as important is a good relationship with the Marshallese.

If confirmed, I will work to maintain the strong relationship between USAKA and the Marshall Islands government and to promote USAKA's beneficial role for affiliated Marshallese communities. The United States and the Marshall Islands also have an important economic relationship. To help achieve the Compact goal of economic self-sufficiency, the United States will provide the government of the RMI [with] over $60 million a year in economic assistance through FY 2023. The majority of this assistance is provided as grants directed toward six sectors: health, education, infrastructure to support health and education, public sector capacity building, private sector development, and the environment.

In addition, U.S. federal agencies operate more than 20 different government programs in the Marshall Islands. Another very important aspect of the Compact is a jointly-managed Trust Fund that will serve as a source of income for the Marshall Islands after annual grant assistance expires in 2023. If confirmed, I will promote economic development and strongly advocate that the Marshallese work vigorously toward economic self-sufficiency, which is one of the primary goals of the Compact, as amended. Maintaining a solid partnership requires work on both sides. Education is a priority sector under the Amended Compact, but more has to be done to prepare young Marshallese for today's global economy. Despite our aid every year, Marshallese citizens are struggling with health issues, unemployment, and social problems. It is in our interest to help the Marshall Islands become more self-reliant and retain their talented and ambitious citizens to foster development and economic growth at home.

As I mentioned, many U.S. government agencies are working to advance those goals. If confirmed, I intend to do everything I can to ensure that our programs are effective in achieving their objectives and will ensure that the inter-agency is also working harmoniously in a "whole of government *approach." If confirmed, I will draw on my experiences from postings throughout the world to work cooperatively with Marshallese officials and society. For example, joint efforts like the Border Liaison Mechanism that I co-chaired with my Mexican counterpart were effective in coordinating policy. In Moscow, as nuclear affairs officer, I coordinated with a range of U.S. agencies to safeguard Russia's nuclear materials. And in negotiating an emergency response agreement with Russia, I forged a close relationship with the Russian negotiator to have that agreement signed and in force to the benefit of both countries.*

If confirmed, I will work closely with colleagues in other Pacific countries to advance U.S. interests regionally. In that spirit I led a counternarcotics team from Tajikistan to Kabul and a business delegation to Kunduz, Afghanistan, to strengthen regional ties to the benefit of the United States in Central Asia. Furthering citizen services, I currently serve as an auxiliary police officer with the New York Police Department in Manhattan and I have assisted Americans in prison in Cuba, Mexico, and Russia. If confirmed, my inter-agency experience will be a critical asset in the RMI, where so many domestic federal agencies – such as the U.S. Postal Service, the Federal Aviation Administration, and the National Weather Service – operate side- by-side with foreign affairs and defense colleagues.

If confirmed, I will work closely with these agencies, and particularly with the Department of the Interior, which has primary responsibility for implementing the Compact's economic provisions, to ensure that assistance efforts are appropriately coordinated and implemented with transparency and accountability. Working in several embassies around the world, I know how critical local staff is to our success. Our mission in the Marshall Islands depends not just on the written text of the Compact of Free Association, but also on creating a bilateral relationship based on partnership and mutual respect between Marshallese and the American people. The Marshallese are great Pacific navigators and I'm sure we can chart a course together.

If confirmed, I will work hard to ensure that my staff has the resources and support it needs to meet our mission in the Marshall Islands. I would like to continue the great work Ambassador Martha Campbell is doing with her staff of 39 officers, local staff, and guards. Thank you for your consideration of my nomination. I welcome any questions you may have.

STEP 21 – FISH AND DRINK BUDWEISER
Majuro, Marshall Islands 2012–2016

I was pretty sure Google maps had made a mistake. The Marshall Islands. Come on, the satellite just showed a little ring of land and thousands of square miles of ocean. Surely, there was supposed to be land in the middle of the ring? Right, the island. The islands. I learned that that's all there is. You can take the whole land mass of the Marshall Islands and put it in Washington, D.C., maybe even Rock Creek Parkway, but then surround it with 700,000 square miles of ocean. Oh, and it is just six feet above sea level on average.

Before allowing me to come as ambassador, the Marshallese, like all host governments, are first asked by diplomatic note if they agree to America's request to send Thomas Hart Armbruster as ambassador. The U.S. seeks *"l' accord,"* the French word for agreement. In this case, the Marshallese had two questions:

Does he drink Budweiser?

Does he fish?

I sent the Department a picture of me fishing, beer in hand, and agreement was at hand. Now, we just needed the Senate to confirm me. The vote came on their last day in session before the summer recess. Kathy and I had already decided that she would stay another year in New York. She had a great job, could walk to work, and her prospects in the Marshall Islands were uncertain. It was painful. New York had been good to us. We played tennis together, took walks in Central Park in the morning, and enjoyed our little one-bedroom apartment on the Upper West Side.

So, I stepped off the United plane after a 4½ hour flight from Honolulu and walked into the VIP room in Majuro. I was met by the foreign minister and the diplomatic corps, there were some drinks, some warm welcomes from the Japanese and Taiwan ambassadors and we were off to the CMR, the Chief of Mission Residence.

So about four years in the Marshall Islands. A very unique place. I had a chance to come full circle to the environmental issues again because that was where the U.S. conducted 67 nuclear tests. There is quite a nuclear legacy that the U.S. is still working on. We addressed that in a lot of different ways. The DOE had programs to monitor radiation and to see what they could do to mitigate the effects of radioactivity in the soil, which is very responsible. They also started giving scholarships to Marshallese students interested in nuclear issues. We had Under Secretary for Arms Control, Rose Gottemoeller, come out and speak on the 60th anniversary of the Castle Bravo nuclear test, really the worst nuclear test, the one that contaminated the Marshallese downwind. She gave an excellent speech. We are always going to be working on that legacy in the Marshall Islands.

We still have very deep security issues there now with the Ronald Reagan Space and Missile Defense base on Kwajalein. That is where missiles launched from Vandenberg Air Base in California land out to the Marshall Islands in the Kwajalein lagoon. The intercontinental missiles are tracked and tested, so the base is a big part of our national security and defense architecture.

Kwajalein was also the scene of some very big WWII battles and there were medals of honor accorded to servicemen, some of whom dove on grenades to save their buddies. So, a lot of history in the Marshall Islands.

Q: *Now what is the population?*

ARMBRUSTER: The population is under 70,000. So, it is very small in terms of population, but it is ¾ of a million square miles of ocean too. It is a very rich fishing area. We have a Compact of Free Association with the Marshallese. They can live, work, and travel in the U.S. and about 35,000 Marshallese live in the U.S., many in Arkansas.

Q: *That is interesting.*

ARMBRUSTER: About $100 million in assistance for education infrastructure and health goes to the Marshall Islands every year. So, we have got a real special relationship with them and I was thinking with sea level rise and climate change we have a real obligation to the Marshallese. One of the big environmental victories for me was nominating Kathy Jetñil-Kijiner, a local poet, to be the civil society speaker at the United Nations climate summit in 2014. She was selected out of hundreds of applicants; that was a big win.

The other thing was that the USS *Prinz Eugen*,[20] a German ship that was anchored in the Marshall Islands where it had been sunk, was still full of oil and I petitioned the Pentagon to have the oil removed.

There were two droughts while I was there, and I declared a disaster both times and sought assistance which I got both times. The U.S. is a responsible partner and a good partner out there, but the Marshallese are going to face some severe problems with climate change because with just a little sea level rise those atolls are under water. We did see that a couple of times where there were inundations. It is pretty precarious for the Marshallese.

Q: *They are all aware of it. Is there anything that can be done relatively easily?*

ARMBRUSTER: No. I guess the one easy thing for the Marshallese is they have the right to work and study in the United States. So many Marshallese live in the United States. In fact, there is a big population in Springdale, Arkansas, many of whom work at the Tyson chicken plant but there are also teachers, policemen, and in government. They are real contributing members of the community. They do have that right to leave the Marshall Islands but if they leave, we lose this culture. It is a great sailing and navigating culture. These were people who could navigate by the wind and just the

---

[20]   https://www.popularmechanics.com/military/navy-ships/a23283428/prinz-eugen-ship-nuked-radioactive-oil/

movement of the waves. They are expert seafarers. They still have their own language, their own songs. The culture is very rich and I think to lose that is to lose something of world heritage.

Q: *They may not have a choice.*

ARMBRUSTER: Especially given that the U.S. has pulled out of the climate accords. That does not bode well. Actually, the Marshallese foreign minister, Tony deBrum, made a really great contribution during the Paris summit to get what they called the "high ambition coalition" together. These were the countries that committed to trying to limit the temperature increase to 1.5° Celsius. That was Tony DeBrum working all night getting these coalitions together.

He told a great story in the UN. He said in Marshallese folklore there was a whale near a beach who was bothering the birds and making all kinds of weird noises. So the birds decided to all take one drop of water in their beaks and the oceans dried up. "Oh," the whale said, "I give up, I give up!" The birds spat the water back and the ocean refilled. The moral is that if you take care of your drop and I take care of my drop and she takes care of her drop we can save the world. I think the Marshallese understand that we have all got to work together to address climate change. They are out front with poetry, with their president, and their diplomacy trying to make the case that this affects everybody and if the Marshall Islands goes under, we all lose.

Q: *I imagine their principal source of income other than U.S. assistance is tourism?*

ARMBRUSTER: No, it is really fish. Fishing is very big. Majuro is one of the top tuna transshipment ports in the world. So if you have a can of tuna there is a pretty good chance it transited the Marshall Islands. They do have great sport fishing. I went marlin fishing with them and the scuba diving is fantastic. We would see sharks and rays and turtles. Nothing against Hawaii, but it was better than

Hawaii. So, tourism might have a chance. The Marshall Islands are four hours west of Honolulu. It is the next stop on the island hopper that goes on to Japan. There may be some scope for tourism in the future. But it is pretty remote and the infrastructure is small, but we have seen Palau just become this incredible dive destination. So, I would think the Marshall Islands has the capability. We did have some great visitors, including Interior Secretary Sally Jewell, and perhaps the greatest sea survivor in history, Jose Salvador Alvarenga, who spent 14 months adrift at sea and finally washed up on the Ebon Atoll.

———◆———

The U.S. military is the No. 2 employer and while fish is the biggest commercial commodity, the public sector is the No. 1 employer. That missile defense base is a real full-time army garrison with scientists, soldiers, and Marshallese staff. Hopefully the U.S.- Marshallese relationship will stay strong to provide further employment opportunities.

The residence is right on the water, lagoon side. Everything in the Marshall Islands is right on the water, but this two-story home, with an apartment below for visitors, sits behind a little pier. From the porch you can look down and see fish schooling. Sometimes, I'd see a family of cuttlefish, with the Papa bear, Mama bear, and little ones. I'd see the jacks slice in and feed on a school of baitfish. And I'd swim from one coral head to the other. Once having a barracuda staring me in the face at the end of a lap, another time seeing a shark far below making his rounds in a leisurely way.

I'd watch the ships come in through the pass in the lagoon on the distance, and watch the sunsets off to the west, past the airport just a few miles down the road. It was a busy lagoon, perhaps the No. 1 port for tuna transshipments. Only a tiny fraction of the revenues went to the Marshallese. The rest went to the Taiwanese, American, and Japanese tuna fleets and the shippers and producers along the way.

The embassy was across the road on the ocean side. The best snorkeling was on that side. Sometimes we'd see spinner dolphins from the embassy balcony. The reef went out a few hundred yards then dropped off and there was a wall of coral where the fish would cruise up and down. It was more dangerous on the ocean side and I'd only go with experienced swimmers, never alone as I did on the lagoon side. Well, almost alone. Skipjack would swim with me for the first 15 minutes, then he'd head for home and shake off and wait for me. He even followed me out when I went scuba diving, but eventually he'd swim home.

Skipjack loved the water

One of the first challenges at the embassy was trying to help a guard. One of our security guards fell off a wall and broke his back. I went to visit him in the Majuro Hospital. He was paralyzed, but conscious and alert. He had to be referred by the Majuro Hospital for treatment off island and to have a chance he had to be accepted somewhere else. I worked with Tripler Hospital, eventually appealing to the administrator of the hospital, arguing that our guard served the United States and deserved a chance to live with an operation at a modern hospital. Tripler came through but our man died before he could board a plane. I went to the funeral, put some money in the basket, sat with the family and listened to the songs they sang to send him on his way.

The guards were real singers. They had a band they called the "Yum Yum Band" and they played some sweet ukulele tunes. They never carried guns, but they were professional and treated every visitor well. One guard swam to work from Ejit, a small islet just off Majuro where many of the Bikini families lived. One loved Skipjack and talked to him whenever he was on guard duty at the residence. They were all good guys and joined in the volleyball games that eventually involved kids from the neighborhood. It was sad to lose one.

It didn't take long watching the sunsets, seeing the albatross glide across the sky, and feeling the tropical breeze on your face to realize that the Marshall Islands, a gentle, peaceful, quiet place, had the misfortune of being the meeting place of two powerful civilizations – American and Japanese – during WWII. The fighting on Kwajalein, Enewetak, and Tarawa was intense, and bullets and mortars still litter the beaches. We brought teams in to clean up some of the battlefields, but even so a woman was killed during my time in the Marshalls by a bullet that was buried in the ground which went off while the woman was cooking. She must be one of the very last casualties of World War Two.

Four Medals of Honor were awarded to Americans who died in WWII battles in the Marshall Islands. I met some of the soldiers who stormed the beaches when they came back for a visit sponsored by the Pentagon. I also met Japanese delegations who came to pay their respects to the dead, and even went to a memorial ceremony when some remains were recovered and returned to the Embassy of Japan. It was clear from the bullet hole that one of the soldiers had been executed. The war in the Pacific was horrific, and the Marshallese suffered as well. Some served as spies, swimming out to American forces to inform them where the Japanese were located. Some Marshallese spies were caught and beheaded.

The Marshallese still contribute to national security, signing up for the U.S. military at a higher rate than any U.S. state. I was happy to help sponsor a young Coast Guard cadet, who took the swimming test in the lagoon in my "backyard" while I served as lifeguard. And the Ronald Reagan Space and Missile

Defense base on Kwajalein renamed one of their ferry boats Solomon Sam, after a Marshallese man who died while serving the U.S. Army in Iraq.

The Space and Missile defense base is where the U.S. tests intercontinental missiles. It's a high-tech Star Wars facility that relies on the Marshallese workforce that comes over every day from Ebeye, one of the most crowded places on Earth.

The Ronald Reagan Space and Missile Defense Facility in action

But the real sacrifice that the Marshallese made toward our security came in the 1950s during the Cold War when 67 nuclear tests were conducted in the Marshall Islands. It's a debt we owe that can never be repaid. The Marshallese gave up an irreplaceable part of themselves with Bikini.

The "Bravo" blast on Bikini

Still, the U.S. contributes to the Marshall Islands through the Compact of Free Association, providing about $100 million in health, education, and infrastructure funding. We also respond when there is a natural disaster, like drought, for example. I asked President Obama for two disaster declarations and he approved assistance from FEMA and USAID both times, sending food, water, and reverse osmosis machines to communities hit by drought.

But the U.S. didn't do much to acknowledge the debt we owed. On March 1st every year the Marshallese have a "Remembrance Day" ceremony, remembering the people who were contaminated when the Castle Bravo test nuclear blast sent radiation to nearby islands. Books can be written about that test. Some would say the timing was deliberate, with the plan being to study the effects of radiation on the Marshallese affected. I never saw evidence that that was true. But the larger issue of a big, powerful country insisting on using a small country for its own protection is incontrovertible. The Marshall Islands was a dot in the global Cold War strategic battlefield. Henry Kissinger is alleged to have said, "There are only 60,000 people there, who gives a damn?" when asked about the effects of the testing on the Marshallese. It's a big issue.

If you think of the Bureau of East Asian and Pacific Affairs (EAP) as a naval fleet, then there are aircraft carriers, like Japan and China; there are battleships, like Korea and Indonesia; and then there are rowboats, like Micronesia, Palau, and the Marshall Islands. We are tiny. And the Department treated us as such. I asked for "three fishing days" a year with the Assistant Secretary. That's how the Marshalls sell fish to other countries, they sell a certain number of days that the foreign fleets buy. I wanted attention from the Seventh floor three times a year, to talk about the nuclear legacy, the Compact of Free Association, sustainable fishing, the epidemic of non-communicable disease, and the existential question of climate change and sea level rise. I got one day. But I made it count.

When a group of ambassadors went to the Pentagon and to Congress, I brought up the Marshall Islands in both meetings. In both, I appealed for help getting oil taken off of the WWII battleship the *Prinz Eugen*. The ship had been towed to Bikini to see how it would survive a nuclear blast. Amazingly, it survived. The ship was towed to Kwajalein and given to the Marshall Islands. It turned over in a storm and sat near the reef, still full of oil, for years. After I left the Marshall Islands, I received a note from Ambassador Karen Stewart, my successor, telling me that the Pentagon had agreed to fund a project sending divers and technicians to offload the oil and protect the reef and the inhabitants of Kwajalein from a catastrophic oil spill. Another good win!

Our embassy motto was "Small but Mighty" referring to a Marshallese folk tale in which the tiniest birds were tethered to a string and launched a mighty oceangoing canoe that the other animals couldn't budge.

My call sign on the radio was "whirlwind," and I tried to keep up a fast pace in what could have been a sleepy post. One of the nicest compliments on my leadership style came from a Regional Security Officer (RSO). He reviewed the film of a fire we'd had. Apparently, some fireworks from next door ignited our tool shed. So, a couple of officers from nearby fought the fire with me and put it out before it could spread or ignite our reserve fuel tanks.

The RSO said to our local guard, "Man, your ambassador is just like Captain Kirk!"

Warp 1, Mr. Sulu…[21]

Because the nuclear legacy still hung so heavily over the relationship, I thought bringing a high-level U.S. official could help restore the balance after decades of mistrust over the issue. I invited Under Secretary for Arms Control and Disarmament, Rose Gottemoeller, now NATO Deputy Secretary, and one of the foremost American National Security professionals for a visit. I was often Rose's control officer in Moscow, and knew she would be tough but on the facts, letting the Marshallese know what the U.S. could and couldn't expect from the U.S. but, most importantly, that she could put the nuclear testing era in historical perspective, and let the Marshallese know that their sacrifice was appreciated. She delivered.

---

[21] Warp Factor – a unitless measurement that represents the speed of a spaceship or something travelling faster than the speed of light. http://www.ex-astris-scientia.org/treknology/warp6.htm

Remarks
Rose Gottemoeller
Majuro, Marshall Islands
March 1, 2014

(As delivered)

I am so honored to be in the Marshall Islands, a nation that the United States sees as our strategic partner, our ally, and our friend. Mr. President, I am honored to be here with such a distinguished group of government, community, and faith leaders, members of the diplomatic corps, and honored guests.

Today, here in this beautiful place, we gather to remember and honor the past, but we also gather in the spirit of community and hope. I would like to second Ambassador Armbruster's message of bromich (condolences); it is the right word for today. The American people remember what took place here and honor the historical and current contributions that the Marshallese people make to help promote peace and stability around the world. For many of you, that means remembering lost family members and loved ones – they are in our thoughts and prayers as well. Today we honor their memory and I know that words can only go so far in healing wounds, but this nation has played an outsized role in the fight for a safer world and for that the United States, and the world, thanks you.

Our commitment to you, solidified by the 1986 Compact and the 2003 Amended Compact, is borne out by our obligation to defend the Marshall Islands and its people, as the United States and its citizens are defended. Of course, the mutual security of our nations is an underlying element of the special relationship between our nations. Marshallese citizens serve with distinction in our armed forces, sharing our commitment to democracy and freedom. I know that the Marshallese rate of enlistment is higher than in most U.S. states. For the Marshallese citizens that have served in Iraq, Afghanistan, and elsewhere in the world, we are so grateful.

On this day – the 60ᵗʰ anniversary of Castle Bravo – and on each and every day, the United States recognizes the effects of its nuclear explosive testing and has accepted and acted on its responsibility. The Department of Energy continues to provide critical medical and environmental programs in the RMI, in addition to improving the provision of such services. In particular, we will continue to work with the local leadership of the four nuclear-affected atolls to assist them in realizing their environmental goals. In this regard, the Department of Energy will be employing the world's best technologies to aid in this endeavor. This, I can assure you, is a promise from the people of the United States.

Since 2004, the United States has provided over $600 million to the Marshall Islands, in the form of direct assistance and subsidies, as well as financial support for rehabilitation of affected atolls, site monitoring, and ongoing health care programs. This year, the U.S. Department of Energy (DOE) initiated a remarkable sponsorship program to increase the science capacity in the Marshall Islands. Two Marshallese students will live and study in the San Francisco Bay Area, including at Lawrence Livermore National Labs (LLNL) itself. The sponsorship pays tuition, room and board, travel, and a living stipend. It also includes a summer internship with LLNL.

As I said at the outset, we are here to remember and honor the past today, but I also want to look to the future with purpose and with hope. In 1962, the Cuban Missile Crisis opened the eyes of the world to the terror of nuclear war, but there were people across the globe who were already all too familiar with nuclear dangers. People in Japan and the Marshall Islands, those downwind from the nuclear test site in Nevada, the mothers who found radioactive material in their children's milk: all understood in first person the health effects of nuclear explosions in the atmosphere. In 1963, about a decade after Castle Bravo, President John F. Kennedy called for a complete ban on nuclear explosive testing.

'The conclusion of such a treaty,' he said, 'so near and yet so far – would check the spiraling arms race in one of its most dangerous areas. It would place the

nuclear powers in a position to deal more effectively with one of the greatest hazards which man faces in 1963 – the further spread of nuclear arms. It would increase our security – it would decrease the prospects of war.'

We are still so near and yet so far from this goal. We were able to achieve part of this objective through the Limited Test-Ban Treaty – banning tests in the water, in space, and in the atmosphere. However, 51 years later, the hazard of the further spread of nuclear weapons remains and we still lack a total ban on nuclear explosive testing. Here again, we should heed President Kennedy's words. 'Surely this goal,' he said, 'is sufficiently important to require our steady pursuit, yielding neither to the temptation to give up the whole effort nor the temptation to give up our insistence on vital and responsible safeguards.'

In 2009, President Obama took up the mantle of the presidents who came before him and laid out his own long-term vision of the peace and security of a world without nuclear weapons. While the United States will and must maintain a safe, secure, and effective nuclear deterrent for as long as nuclear weapons exist, we have properly refocused our nuclear policy for the 21st century. As outlined in the 2010 Nuclear Posture Review (NPR), we are now on a path that confronts the threats we face today and those on the near horizon. This allows us to work with allies and partners to pursue arms control and disarmament measures that can lead us down the path toward a nuclear-free world.

Mindful of the devastating human consequences of nuclear war, the United States has also clearly stated that it is in our interest, and that of all other nations, that the nearly 70-year record of non-use of nuclear weapons be extended forever. We also concluded that the time for a complete and total ban on nuclear explosive testing is long overdue. U.S. ratification of the Comprehensive Nuclear-Test-Ban Treaty (CTBT) is a pivotal part of this effort.

Ratification of the CTBT is central to leading other nuclear weapons states toward a world of diminished reliance on nuclear weapons, reduced nuclear competition, and eventual nuclear disarmament. The United

States now maintains a safe, secure, and effective nuclear arsenal through our science-based Stockpile Stewardship program without nuclear explosive testing, which the United States halted in 1992.

The United States will be patient in our pursuit of ratification, but we will also be persistent. It has been a long time since the CTBT was on the front pages of newspapers, so we will need time to make the case for this Treaty. Together, we can work through questions and concerns about the Treaty and explosive nuclear testing. Our answers to those questions continue to grow stronger with the proven and increasing capabilities of the Stockpile Stewardship program and the verification system of the Treaty, including the International Monitoring System.

I cannot emphasize strongly enough that it is precisely our deep under-standing of the consequences of nuclear weapons – including the dangerous health effects of nuclear explosive testing – that has guided and motivated our efforts to reduce and ultimately eliminate these most dangerous and awe-inspiring weapons. Entry into force of the CTBT is one such essential part of our pragmatic, step-by-step approach to eliminating nuclear dangers. The Treaty will make the world a safer place for the Marshall Islands, the United States, for every nation around the globe.

This is not just a security issue; this is an issue of humanity, of health, of morality. We are the stewards of this Earth and we owe it to those who have fallen – to those who suffer still – to work together, one step at a time, until nuclear explosive testing is banned worldwide, getting us one step closer to our goal of the peace and security of a world without nuclear weapons. In closing, I want to reiterate that the United States and the world owe the Marshallese a debt of gratitude. The RMI has been a leader in countering climate change, a contributor to international security, and our partner on global issues. Together, we can and should continue to work for what President Kennedy called 'a genuine peace, the kind of peace that makes life on Earth worth living.'

Finally, I can only say kommol tata! Thank you!

Mar 3, 2014 – Under Secretary of State for Arms Control and International Security, Rose Gottemoeller, and U.S. Ambassador to the Marshall Islands, Tom Armbruster, greet children on Kili Island on March 3, 2014. Under Secretary Gottemoeller and Ambassador Armbruster participated in Remembrance Day ceremonies in the Marshall Islands

Rose's visit was significant. She was the highest-ranking U.S. visitor since George Schultz stopped over from an Asian trip. And she said all the right things. Rose also went to Kili, the island where many Bikinians wound up after a long and hard odyssey through the Marshall Islands.[22] The visit looked like it was going to lead to something even more significant; increased funding. Rose believed that the Marshall Islands had not been given due compensation for the

22   Kili Island was the place where the original Bikinians were resettled after a disastrous stay on another island that had no resources. It has been a long, hard odyssey for the people of Bikini. Now, many have resettled in the U.S. but Kili remains the most important Marshallese community of people from Bikini and their descendants, many of whom have never seen the beautiful island of Bikini.

nuclear tests and asked the embassy to develop a list of projects that the United States could fund. There was no end to possibilities.

Then, unluckily, Foreign Minister Tony deBrum decided to sue the United States for breach of the Nuclear Non-Proliferation Treaty. The Under-Secretary's initiative ended, and all the possibilities went up in smoke. It was disappointing, but I knew her visit and a real breakthrough was a longshot. I hoped her visit would signal a greater recognition on the part of the U.S. for the Marshall Islands' sacrifice in the Cold War, but I did not expect anything more. The fact that she wanted to take the ball further was her initiative and it shows how important it is, especially if you are serving in a remote, far post, to get the big bosses out to visit. It is the only way to make your post real to them and not just a dot on the map. In any case, I was grateful that we got the visit.

We almost had a visit from Secretary of State John Kerry. He was planning to come on his way back from a tour of Asia, just like Schultz. We mapped out a plan and were ready for a good, short visit to highlight climate change and the need for action. I had also once planned a big nuclear city tour for John Kerry when he was still a senator. I was in Moscow and had been tasked as control officer – tasked or volunteered, I forget which. I had a good program set up but then the war in Kosovo heated up and relations between the U.S. and Russia went south, permanently as it turns out. Ironically, Secretary Kerry's visit to the Marshall Islands was also put off by conflict. Another opportunity missed.

But, somehow or other, the Marshall Islands manages to make it on the news. The castaway, Jose Salvador Alvarenga, drifted onto the Marshall Islands and my deputy and I happened to both speak Spanish. We interviewed him onboard the Marshallese patrol boat, just after it pulled into the dock in Majuro, and reported our interview to the authorities. Jose Salvador Alvarenga claims he survived 13 months lost at sea after leaving Mexico, washing up on Marshall Islands.

A castaway from Mexico who identified himself as Jose Salvador Alvarenga walks with the help of a nurse in Majuro, Marshall Islands, after a 22-hour boat ride from isolated Ebon Atoll, Feb. 3, 2014 (GETTY)

We both came away believing that his story of being blown off course from a coastal Mexican fishing village to the Marshall Islands was true. The part that really rang true to me was when he said a container ship came by and he waved for help and they just waved back and kept going. You could feel the heartbreak in his voice and tell that this was not something one would just make up. His story of drinking bird's blood and fishing to stay alive all seemed true. I suppose he is one of the world's greatest survivors, which is what I told CNN when interviewed.

Castaway Jose Salvador Alvarenga's boat that kept him alive for 438 days

(U.S. Embassy Majuro Photo)

Jose Salvador Alvarenga, a castaway from Mexico steps off the *Lomor* Sea Patrol vessel in Majuro, Marshall Islands, with the help of a nurse, Feb. 3, 2014 (GETTY)

WELLINGTON, New Zealand – *It's a story that almost defies belief: A man leaves Mexico in December 2012 for a day of shark fishing and ends up surviving 13 months on fish, birds and turtles before washing ashore on the remote Marshall Islands some 5,500 miles away.*

But that's the story a man identifying himself as 37-year-old Jose Salvador Alvarenga told the U.S. ambassador in the Marshall Islands and the nation's officials during a 30-minute meeting Monday before he was taken to a local hospital for monitoring. Alvarenga washed ashore on the tiny atoll of Ebon in the Pacific Ocean last week before being taken to the capital, Majuro, on Monday.

'It's hard for me to imagine someone surviving 13 months at sea,' said Ambassador Tom Armbruster in Majuro. 'But it's also hard to imagine how someone might arrive on Ebon out of the blue. Certainly this guy has had an ordeal and has been at sea for some time.'

Other officials were reacting cautiously to the Spanish-speaking man's story while they try to piece together more information. If true, the man's ordeal would rank among the greatest tales ever of survival at sea.

Armbruster said the soft-spoken man complained of joint pain Monday and had a limp but was able to walk. He had long hair and a beard, the ambassador said, and rather than appearing emaciated he looked puffy in places, including around his ankles. Otherwise, he added, Alvarenga seemed in reasonable health.

Armbruster, who speaks Spanish, said the survivor told the following story:

He's a native of El Salvador but has lived in Mexico for 15 years and fishes for a man he knows as Willie, catching sharks for 25 pesos ($1.90) per pound.

On Dec. 21, 2012, Alvarenga left Mexico in his 23-foot fiberglass boat for a day's fishing, accompanied by a teen he knew only as Ezekiel, who was between 15 and 18.

A storm blew the fishermen off course, and soon they were lost and adrift.

'He talked about scooping up little fish that swam alongside the boat and eating them raw,' Armbruster said. 'He also said he ate birds and drank birds' blood.' After about a month, Ezekiel died, the survivor told officials.

Alvarenga also talked about eating turtles. Once near Ebon, he swam ashore.

'He thanked God, initially, that he had survived,' the ambassador said. 'He's very anxious to get back in touch with his employer, and also with the family of Ezekiel. That's his driving motivation at the moment.'

Armbruster said the man said he had no family in Mexico, but he does have three brothers who live in the U.S., although he could not immediately provide officials with contact details.

Gee Bing, the acting secretary of foreign affairs for the Marshall Islands, said he was somewhat skeptical of Alvarenga's account after meeting with him Monday.

'It does sound like an incredible story and I'm not sure if I believe his story,' Bing said. 'When we saw him, he was not really thin compared to other survivors in the past. I may have some doubts. Once we start communicating with where he's from, we'll be able to find out more information.'

Bing said the man had no identification with him and other details of his story remained sketchy, including the exact location of his departure from Mexico.

The survivor's vital signs appeared good except that his blood pressure was a bit low, Bing said. After doctors give him the all-clear, Bing said, officials hope to repatriate him to Mexico or whatever country is appropriate. Bing said the Mexican ambassador in the Philippines, Julio Camarena, has been involved in the case. Camarena could not be contacted immediately.

Erik van Sebille, a Sydney-based oceanographer at the University of New South Wales, said there was a good chance a boat drifting off Mexico's west coast would eventually be carried by currents to the Marshall Islands. He said such a journey would typically take 18 months to two years depending on the winds and currents, although 13 months was possible.

172

'The way that the currents in the Pacific work is that there is a very strong westerly current just north of the equator and that basically drives you directly from Mexico all the way toward Indonesia and in the path, you go right over the Marshall Islands,' he said.

There have been other cases of people surviving for months adrift in the Pacific. In a case with similarities, three Mexican shark fishermen in 2006 said they were lost at sea for nine months before being rescued near the Marshall Islands. In 1989, four men survived nearly four months in the Pacific Ocean near New Zealand after their multi-hulled boat capsized.

While we are talking about fantastic journeys, let me put my two cents in about Amelia

Earhart. There's a chain of custody, or of witness testimony, that leads me to believe that Amelia Earhart and Fred Noonan crash-landed on Mili Island in the Marshall Islands, were put on a boat bound for Jaluit, still in the Marshalls, and then taken to Saipan and executed. The story is so well established in the Marshalls that there are even postage stamps depicting Amelia's plane crash landing on Mili.

The only problem with the narrative is that it relies on Marshallese eyewitnesses. For the Marshallese, there is no question. The witnesses are reliable, they had no reason to lie, and stood to gain nothing. If anything, there was a disincentive for speaking out. The story goes that a doctor who treated Noonan was later killed by the Japanese, perhaps for what he knew. But the outside world seems to want more. The competing theory relies on "bones" found on Nikumaroro that are no longer available to science. For me, it's Mili-Jaluit-Saipan. There should be an "Amelia's Hideaway" bar in Majuro with Amelia era artifacts and photos.

Coach Tom Newell is normally unstoppable. You put him on a basketball court with close to 100 kids and by the end of practice he'll know their names. He'll know who would have a shot at a big-time university. He'll know what the embassy wants to communicate, and he'll work it into his routine, or he'll call on the embassy officer, sometimes me, to put a word in on nutrition, or staying in school, or staying off of tobacco. I knew I wanted Tom to come to the Marshall Islands given the high rates of diabetes. Amputation is the No. 1 surgical procedure at the Majuro Hospital, and it's all thanks to the "Western diet" which I, even as a Westerner, could not really digest. Lots of white rice, spam, turkey tails, junk food, and soda. An island diet of fish, coconut, taro and pandanus would actually be hard to beat and the Marshallese can be as fit and healthy as anyone on the planet, but the cheap junk food was killing them.

It was disconcerting to see Tom get off the plane for his annual tour of the Marshalls looking less than ideal. I greeted him at the airport.

"Tom, *Iokwe*, welcome back. Hey, you've got a radio interview coming up."

"Aw, Tommy, I'm hurting. I've got to get to the doc!"

"You're kidding. What's going on?"

"Kidney stone. Just started acting up on the plane."

So, we got Tom to the hospital and they did some tests. That night, unbeknownst to me, he snuck out of the downstairs apartment, got the guard to hail a ride, and reported into hospital, in pain. Our General Services Officer, Russell, got a call from the guard and he went into the hospital too at midnight. That happened three nights in a row with no improvement.

I told the foreign minister at an event that I thought I was going to have to send Tom back home. It would be disappointing to the kids, but I was getting worried, although Tom is just about unbreakable. Foreign Minister deBrum said, "Don't worry. Ramsey Reimers makes a potion, a uh, medicine. It'll fix him right up."

That night the potion arrived at the guard house. It was aloe and a lot of other native plants mashed up. I never got the full recipe. Tom drank it down. He did that three times and the kidney stone passed. I saw Foreign Minister deBrum right away and told him. "It worked!?" he said, shocked. I guess we should get that recipe to the food and drug administration.

Basketball is big in the Marshall Islands

Former NBA Coach Tom Newell always brings his A-game to Public Diplomacy events, teaching kids basketball basics as well as important life lessons.

Tom showing us how it's done

There were a lot of great ways to support good nutrition in the Marshall Islands. There was the Wellness Center run by the Canvasback NGO out of San Francisco. They served healthy meals, checked your blood sugar, put you on a diet plan, and had yoga and exercise classes, not to mention a garden to grow fresh veggies.

We sponsored an ambassador's Garden Prize for schools with the U.S., Taiwanese, and Japanese ambassadors all visiting schools, eating hot peppers, and giving out prizes and garden implements to the winners. There was a triathlon we co-sponsored and there was the Japanese relay known as Ekkiden. That race went the length of the island and back!

Photo finish for Ambassador Anzai and me

Drought was one indication of climate change in the Marshall Islands and it can be devastating for a community. Most Marshallese get their water from rainwater, either in home catchments or in reservoirs. In Majuro, the reservoir sits at the end of the airport and the runway serves as a conveyor for rain. Since the runway is a nice long, hard surface the rain can be directed to the reservoir and used for the general population. The reservoir's capacity is listed on a website, so people know if the reservoir is getting low. Many people have their own backyard rain catchments systems too. Majuro also has a problem with wastewater. A sewer outfall, built by a company in the American Midwest, failed almost immediately and so sewage goes directly into the sea, rather than being piped safely offshore. I worked with the Department of the Interior to get an outfall funded that could withstand strong ocean currents.

Keeping coral healthy is essential for an island community. Coral is even mined for construction projects, as companies attempt to get to the sand under the coral. We relocated some coral near the airport to try to save it, but it's an uphill battle. I remember the little fish that lived in the coral would stay right with it, even when we broke it off to transport it. That's their home.

One American researcher felt so strongly about the Marshall Islands' coral policy he ended up getting tossed in jail. We visited him and brought a fan. Then he went on a hunger strike from about 9:30 to 3:30 in the afternoon when he was released. Sounds funny, but coral is life for tropical islands. Especially if you want people to eat a healthy local diet.

An Interview with Ambassador Thomas Hart Armbruster, U.S. Ambassador to the Marshall Islands

To learn more about the U.S. Embassy to the Marshall Islands, visit http://majuro.usembassy.gov/

By AARON MAK
August 15, 2013

THOMAS HART ARMBRUSTER became Ambassador to the Republic of the Marshall

Islands (RMI) on August 16, 2012. Previously, Armbruster held the position of Diplomat in

Residence in New York City, and he has also served on behalf of the U.S. government in Afghanistan, Cuba, Finland, Mexico, Russia, and Tajikistan. He earned his bachelor's degree from McDaniel College in Westminster, MD as well as master's degrees from St. Mary's University and the Naval War College.

The Politic: Is there one experience, person, or event in the RMI that has greatly influenced one or more of your policies? How so?

Right now what we are really working on in the Marshall Islands is a response to the drought in the northern islands and atolls. About 6,000 people are affected. Yesterday, I released another $100,000 from a joint U.S.-Marshallese fund for drought response. We are waiting to see if the Marshalls will ask President Obama for additional assistance. We had a team here from FEMA, the U.S. Department of Agriculture, and USAID assessing the damages of the drought. We have worked very well with the Marshalls. We can contribute further if they ask for it.

The Politic: Can you talk about how the citizens of the RMI are coping with the drought and how the US is providing assistance?

The response so far has centered on getting water to the affected islands. They are doing that with reverse osmosis machines and with water bladders [large tanks of water]. The U.S. Department of Agriculture is looking at long-term ways to deal with it, maybe with more drought resistant crops or different ways of irrigation. They are trying to look at it in the long term so that we can address not just the short-term drought but also make this community a bit more resilient to drought in the first place.

The Politic: In your testimony before the Senate Foreign Relations Committee you claim, "The Marshall Islands is a key partner in the United States' deepening commitment to the Pacific." Can you elaborate on what the Marshall Islands' role is in this commitment?

In terms of national security, the U.S. Army base Kwajalein Atoll (USAKA) is really a jewel.

It is our space and missile defense center where they test rockets launched from Vandenberg Air Force base into the Kwajalein area. It is an army base with a lot of scientists involved and they're doing work not just on missile defense but also on tracking of space debris. They have had NASA there sending up sounding rockets [which carry instruments to make scientific measurements] and doing tests on the upper atmosphere. So it is an active army base with a unique role to play. I am very happy that the Marshalls host USAKA. USAKA is the No. 2 employer in the country. It is also a place where some Marshallese go to school, and those students have done quite well. They have become leaders in the government.

Marshall Islands children

The Politic: In your testimony to the Senate Foreign Relations Committee, you claimed that even though we send aid every year to the RMI, students are still struggling with health, education, and unemployment. What do you think needs to change, if anything, with respect to our aid to the Marshall Islands?

We have to keep at it. I think getting the Peace Corps here could help with the English scores. We have just seen some data from the College of the Marshall Islands indicating that entrants to the college are doing better on their tests — their English is better. Students come to the college better prepared if they start to learn English earlier. They are going to be more successful. We have worked closely with the Education Minister and were very impressed with the students' dedication. As long as the U.S. and the Marshalls have an agreement that health and education are two of the top priorities, then we will continue to find ways to improve. But it is an ongoing process and one that it important for the Marshallese whether they decide to stay here [in the Marshall Islands] or come to the United States, which they can do under the Compact of Free Association.

The other thing we have really pushed is access to the Coast Guard Academy, which Marshallese citizens can get into for free. They have built foundations, learning engineering skills and leadership skills. We also have a lot of Marshallese who join the military and they come back with training and skills from those experiences as well.

The Politic: Can you briefly discuss how the 1986 Compact of Free Association functions today?

The Compact provides almost $70 million in assistance through the Department of the Interior, mostly in health, education, and infrastructure. We also have 20 U.S. government agencies outside of the Department of the Interior involved with the Marshalls. The Compact allows the U.S. to provide for the defense of the Marshall Islands; they are committed to our defense as well. And then we have payments that continue until the year 2023, which decrease every year. We worked very hard on a strategy to deal with the decrease in payments, so that the money is supplemented by revenues to the state.

We also contribute to a trust fund that will help the Marshalls continue operations after the payments from the Compact end. That trust fund this year is actually doing quite well. I think it is up to something like $180 million. The goal is to have $700 million by 2023. It is being managed by financial firms that diversify the fund, and we are hopeful that it will contribute to the Marshalls' income, along with fisheries and other sectors of the economy.

The Politic: Is financial independence for the Marshall Islands a goal that the U.S. is working toward?

These days, I think — and the Marshalls will say this themselves — that every country in this globalized world is dependent on one another. So I am not sure we could say "completely independent." We do have long-lasting ties with the Marshalls, so we are not going to walk away in 2023 and say, "good luck." The army base agreement that we have is until 2066, with an option to extend that agreement. "Independence" is not quite the word, but certainly more self-sufficiency is the right goal. We are trying to see their enterprises operate more efficiently, such as the energy companies and the airlines. Those are the challenges we are trying to address.

The Politic: Phillip Muller, the foreign minister of the RMI, wrote an op-ed piece in the Washington Post attributing the drought and the rising of sea levels to climate change from carbon emissions. Can you discuss what the general feeling on climate change is in the RMI and your thoughts on their position?

The RMI is definitely one of the most vulnerable countries in the world as most of Majuro is at best six to eight feet above sea level. In order to address climate change and adaptation, the State Department has funded a climate change advisor here for the last couple of years, a man named Steve Why. It is obviously the type of question where there is no easy answer. The way we are contributing is by providing experts — not just statewide but also coastal management experts — who can come here and look at ways to prevent erosion and restore coral reefs. Coral reefs are a defense against rising sea levels. We look for ways to contribute. It is an important problem throughout all of the Pacific and is something that we are working on regionally. I know it is something Secretary Kerry is also quite concerned about. We welcome the dialog on that.

The Politic: The U.S. performed 67 tests of nuclear weapons in the Marshall Islands from 1946 to 1958. Can you talk about the consequences of those tests and what the U.S. has done in the 21st century to help remedy their harmful effects?

There is a Department of Energy Program that screens people who were exposed to radiation, especially in the Atoll Bravo test. That screening goes on for life. It is not just for radiation-related cancers, but health screening in general. That is something the U.S. has committed to and will continue to do. We continue to talk to the Marshalls about the nuclear testing era, which is a very important issue for them. We are going to hand over this month a thousand pages of recently declassified documents about the testing era. We have provided for a Remembrance Day, which is an annual commemoration of the Atoll Bravo test at the College of the Marshall Islands. The United States has provided full and final compensation; this is an issue that we are happy to engage in. Additionally, the Department of Energy is looking at perhaps a scholarship to bring more Marshalls into the sciences so that they can look at this issue independently, and I think that is a good initiative as well.

The Politic: Do you sense any resentment on the part of the citizens of the RMI concerning the tests?

It is hard for me to characterize how the Marshallese feel about it. It may be somewhat of a generational thing as well. I know that it is something school kids still talk about. It is part of their history and part of our shared history. It depends on the person. Some people feel very strongly about it. The overall relationship between the Marshall Islands and the U.S. is one of friendship, respect, and a mutual outlook on the world. We share a lot of values and we certainly share a lot of history and relationships. Many Marshallese are now working in the United States. So it is a very rich and deep relationship.

The Politic: On that note, how do you feel that America is represented abroad, and are there any elements of American foreign policy that you would want to change?

I think we have done better in connecting with youth, and not just dealing with the government elite, the foreign ministry, and so on. We really do try to get out. We had an NBA coach here, which was our secret weapon to talk to kids about nutrition and exercise. We had a musical band that connected immediately with local audiences. We have realized that the means embassies can use to get Americans – whether they are citizens, musicians, or artists – to make those connections are a really critical part of diplomacy.

I loved diving with Hiro, the owner of Ray Crew Diving in the Marshalls. My most memorable dive, certainly not my best, was at one of our usual spots, the "aquarium." It was an hour or so around the lagoon to the pass to the ocean and was the opposite of a drift dive – a drift dive drops you off, the current takes you and you drift with it and get picked up "downwind." In this dive, we get dropped off and kick like crazy against the current as we descend, then we get to the bottom about 60 to 100 feet down and hang on to something and watch the show. This time, I was the show.

First, I cut my thumb and I was bleeding green blood, thanks to whatever chemistry makes it green down there. Then, a shark swam by, looked at me with disdain, like "Tourist! Geez!" He swam away, but then my right lens popped out of my mask. My mask filled with water and I had to rely on my eyesight through sea water. Not cool. Hiro's assistant, Sato, an extremely able diver, came to the rescue and offered his mask. I wore it for a while and then decided he had greater responsibilities with the rest of the day's party, so I gave it back to him and put mine back on.

Remarkably, if I covered the right eye with my hand, I could somewhat keep a clear line of sight – well, a blurry line of sight. We finished the dive. Afterwards, Hiro said, "Tom-san, we were wondering, ah, could we, keep your mask, as a memento to today?" I was a little embarrassed by the whole thing and said, "No, I guess I'll try to fix it." Heck, if I still have that somewhere, Hiro-san, it's yours. And if you see that shark, tell him I'll be better prepared next time.

This was our first viral Embassy Majuro Facebook post. A flying fish or *jojo* in Marshallese. Our followers loved kids, the military, and fish!

This photo perfectly describes an "unok," the Marshallese word for the bird feeding frenzy that occurs when the big fish start forcing the little fish to the surface.

STEP 22 – CONNECT YOUR WORK TO THE WORLD
Still Majuro, Marshall Islands 2012–2016

But coral, drought, wastewater technology, and nutrition are just issues on the margin of the big climate change challenge, sea level rise. At just six feet above sea level on average, the Marshall Islands is one of the two or three most vulnerable countries in the world to sea level rise. We had already seen inundations due to "king tides" when the moon and ocean swells converged to flood Majuro. But the kind of sea level rise that they predict with just a few degrees of global warming centigrade could sink the Marshalls and with it their culture, their language, the Space and Missile Defense base and the underground repository of nuclear waste at Runit Dome.

There have been fears that Runit Dome is going to be flooded and contaminate the Pacific, but I don't think this will happen. Although it's a symbol of the Cold War and of the inadequate clean up to date, I don't think it is the scary ticking time bomb that is sometimes portrayed in the press.

The Runit Dome Nuclear Waste Repository on Enewetak

But let's start with the Marshallese themselves and Kathy Jetñil-Kijiner's poem *Tell Them*. I submitted the poem to the United Nations and nominated her to be the Civil Society Speaker for the UN's Climate Summit in New York in

2014. I knew about the opportunity because John Webster was doing another climate film. His first, *Recipes for Disaster*, featured him and his family living without oil-based products for a year. No gas, no plastic, no jet fuel. The next film was called *Little Yellow Boots*, featuring the world as he imagined it for his great granddaughter, in a post climate change world. Johnny asked if I knew any Marshallese who would be good for the film and he told me about the United Nations global search for a voice for climate. I told him about Kathy Jetñil-Kijiner.

Kathy was teaching at the Marshall Islands College and our intern got her final documents and signatures the last day of eligibility and we mailed off the nomination. She was one of over 500 applicants for the worldwide search for the voice of climate change:

04/13/11

POEM: TELL THEM

Tell Them

I prepared the package

for my friends in the states

the dangling earrings woven

into half moons black pearls glinting

like an eye in a storm of tight spirals

the baskets

sturdy, also woven

brown cowry shells shiny

intricate mandalas

shaped by calloused fingers

Inside the basket

a message:

Wear these earrings

to parties

to your classes and meetings to the grocery store, the corner store

and while riding the bus

Store jewelry, incense, copper coins and curling letters like this one

in this basket

and when others ask you

where you got this

you tell them

they're from the Marshall Islands

show them where it is on a map

tell them we are a proud people toasted dark brown as the carved ribs of a tree stump

tell them we are descendents

of the finest navigators in the world tell them our islands were dropped from a basket

carried by a giant

tell them we are the hollow hulls

of canoes as fast as the wind

slicing through the pacific sea

we are wood shavings

and drying pandanus leaves

and sticky bwiros at kemems

tell them we are sweet harmonies

of grandmothers mothers aunties and sisters songs late into night

tell them we are whispered prayers

the breath of God

a crown of fushia flowers encircling

aunty mary's white sea foam hair

tell them we are styrofoam cups of koolaid red waiting patiently for the ilomij

tell them we are papaya golden sunsets bleeding into a glittering open sea

we are skies uncluttered

majestic in their sweeping landscape

we are the ocean

terrifying and regal in its power

tell them we are dusty rubber slippers

swiped

from concrete doorsteps

we are the ripped seams

and the broken door handles of taxis

we are sweaty hands shaking another sweaty hand in heat tell them

we are days

and nights hotter

than anything you can imagine

tell them we are little girls with braids

cartwheeling beneath the rain

we are shards of broken beer bottles

burrowed beneath fine white sand

we are children flinging

like rubber bands

across a road clogged with chugging cars

tell them

we only have one road

and after all this

tell them about the water

how we have seen it rising

flooding across our cemeteries gushing over the sea walls

and crashing against our homes

tell them what it's like to see the entire ocean___level___with the land

tell them

we are afraid

tell them we don't know

of the politics

or the science

but tell them we see

what is in our own backyard

tell them that some of us

are old fishermen who believe that God

made us a promise

some of us

are more skeptical of God but most importantly tell them

we don't want to leave

we've never wanted to leave

and that we

are nothing without our islands.

"We've never wanted to leave." That refers to the evacuation of Bikini, and the fact that although King Juda of Bikini told the Navy "It is in God's Hands," the use of the Marshalls as a testing ground was a foregone conclusion.

The Foreign Service is an up or out system. At about this time I was hoping to get an onward assignment but first needed a promotion to Minister Counselor. I was already in the Senior Foreign Service but needed to move up one more rank to stay in the game.

I was the European bureau's candidate to be ambassador to Georgia following the Marshalls, a job I would have loved, but the DCM committee turned me down. With only one tour in Washington, I was missing a check mark in that box and neither did I have a tour in Afghanistan or Iraq. So chances were not great, although I had 4/4 in a language, leadership positions in four bureaus, good performance reviews, and top scores for leadership from Embassy Majuro staff, I needed more.

When she was visiting the Marshall Islands, Under Secretary Gottemoeller asked what had happened in Vladivostok with the man who was paralyzed and seeking compensation. I told her the story. She said, "So you didn't try to keep him from getting compensation?" I almost laughed, "No." I said, knowing that I was the one who started the whole compensation movement. Somehow, word had got back to Washington that I was trying to block it. An ambassador earlier told me, "You need to get yourself known in Washington!" More good advice.

There was one more opportunity. About two years into the Majuro tour I was asked if I could take an immediate opening as Consul General in St Petersburg, Russia. The "needs of the service" were pretty clear and it was Rose who told me that Deputy Secretary Burns, who had been ambassador in Moscow, thought I would be good for the job.

Kathy had her library underway in Majuro and leaving early would have meant not seeing that project through. Or we could live apart until she finished her project. Kathy's job had come second so many times. At one juncture the Department said Kathy was not qualified for a librarian job, so there was no love lost between the Department and Kathy. Spousal employment remains a huge factor for foreign service officers and the lack of career opportunity for spouses is the No. 1 reason people leave the Foreign Service.

I was in Honolulu for a meeting, trying to juggle the St Petersburg request and a Compact of

Free Association meeting. I went on a long run. In fact, Kathy was also training for the Honolulu marathon, and curtailing would have put an end to the run in December. I ran and ran and came to the conclusion that family came first in this instance and dashed off an email saying 'No.'

When I got to my first meeting that morning, I felt like I had pretty much killed my career with that email. Before saying 'no' the idea of getting back to Russia, being part of something that the bureau and the whole department viewed as relevant was exciting, and I was already imagining how I could engage with youth and energize the relationship. The day before I turned it down Kathy and I had been pretty high on it and it looked like we'd do it. So the last hope to keep my Foreign Service career going was to get promoted out of the Marshall Islands.

If I had gone to St Petersburg, I might have missed the opportunity to nominate Kathy Jetnil-Kijiner to address world leaders at the 2014 Climate Summit in New York. That would not have been a good trade! Kathy proved to be an inspiring speaker and her performance has resonated over the years. When Kathy Jetñil-Kijiner was selected to be the UN Civil Society Speaker from more than 500 candidates, she brought the United Nations General Assembly to their feet, the first standing ovation since Nelson Mandela addressed the world leaders. She took that opportunity and made the most of it, making her country proud and touching people in a way the scientists and politicians never could. She also anchored the end of Johnny's film, with one UN official saying she would remember Kathy's performance for the rest of her life.

Kathy Jetñil-Kijiner at the United Nations (Sep 23, 2014).

UNITED NATIONS CLIMATE SUMMIT OPENING CEREMONY – A POEM TO MY DAUGHTER[23]

dear matafele peinam,

you are a seven month old sunrise of gummy smiles

you are bald as an egg and bald as the buddha

you are thighs that are thunder and shrieks that are lightning

so excited for bananas, hugs and

our morning walks past the lagoon

dear matafele peinam,

i want to tell you about that lagoon

that lucid, sleepy lagoon lounging against the sunrise

men say that one day

that lagoon will devour you

---

23   https://jkijiner.wordpress.com/2014/09/24/united-nations-climate-summit-opening-ceremo-ny-my-poem-to-my-daughter/

they say it will gnaw at the shoreline

chew at the roots of your breadfruit trees

gulp down rows of your seawalls

and crunch your island's shattered bones

they say you, your daughter

and your granddaughter, too

will wander rootless

with only a passport to call home

dear matafele peinam,

don't cry

mommy promises you

no one

will come and devour you

no greedy whale of a company sharking through political seas

no backwater bullying of businesses with broken morals

no blindfolded bureaucracies gonna push

this mother ocean over

the edge

no one's drowning, baby

no one's moving

no one's losing

their homeland

no one's gonna become

a climate change refugee

or should i say

no one else

to the carteret islanders of papua new guinea

and to the taro islanders of the solomon islands

i take this moment

to apologize to you

we are drawing the line here

because baby we are going to fight

your mommy daddy

bubu jimma your country and president too

we will all fight

and even though there are those

hidden behind platinum titles

who like to pretend

that we don't exist

that the marshall islands

tuvalu

kiribati

maldives

and typhoon haiyan in the philippines

and floods of pakistan, algeria, colombia

and all the hurricanes, earthquakes, and tidal waves

didn't exist

still

there are those

who see us

hands reaching out

fists raising up

banners unfurling

megaphones booming

and we are

canoes blocking coal ships

we are

the radiance of solar villages

we are

the rich clean soil of the farmer's past

we are

petitions blooming from teenage fingertips

we are

families biking, recycling, reusing,

engineers dreaming, designing, building,

artists painting, dancing, writing

and we are spreading the word

and there are thousands out on the street

marching with signs

hand in hand

chanting for change NOW

and they're marching for you, baby

they're marching for us

because we deserve to do more than just

survive

we deserve

to thrive

dear matafele peinam,

you are eyes heavy

with drowsy weight

so just close those eyes, baby

and sleep in peace

because we won't let you down

you'll see

That optimism, and the belief that together we can make a difference was what moved me. I remember watching the UN stream from Majuro at midnight in bed. It was a beautiful moment. Kathy whispered to her husband after the reading, "I messed up!" She bobbled a word here or there and thought the standing ovation was the delegation being polite. She didn't know it was the world being bowled over. It is sometimes hard for her to keep that optimism I know.

And I've been hoping Kathy will don scuba gear and become a poetic force for coral as she sees first-hand the beauty of the Marshall Islands underwater. But, with her mother, Hilda Heine, current president of the Marshall Islands, I know this fight is far from over and I hope that the United States will stand with the Marshall Islands to mitigate climate change and one day put the world on a sustainable path forward, for the sake of Matafele Penem and for the rest of us.

There is a long line of what we would today call activists from the Marshall Islands, among them, Darlene Keju, who first talked openly about the pain nuclear testing was causing her people and who later died of cancer herself, and Tony deBrum, who was a lifelong advocate for many causes. He created the world's largest shark sanctuary, he battled everyone on nuclear issues, having seen the Bravo blast at age nine, and perhaps his greatest battle, and victory, was climate change. He was the engineer of the "High Ambition Coalition" in Paris, that sought the most aggressive climate targets. I battled with Tony sometimes on policy issues, but I respected him and loved to hear his stories of the old days. Like how communities would draw dolphins in toward shore, knocking rocks under the water to attract them, and how they would all jump as one on shore once the queen dolphin gave the signal. He had a million stories and there were many late nights where he would reminisce and hold court. And if there was kava[24] nearby, Tony was just fine with that. I tried it once, didn't do anything for me, and I avoided it after that. I heard you really got a free pass the first time, but after that it could have a paralyzing effect. I'm pretty much anti-drugs or alcohol in anything but minimum amounts. I figure I need all the faculties I've got and then some. Tony also had a distinctive voice that I can still hear. He was a great man and died, from cancer, in 2017.

Although I am an environmentalist, I must admit I like fishing. Tommy Kijiner, Kathy Jetñil-Kijiner's dad, would take me out on his boat. We never had a lot of luck, mostly jacks, but he would eat the beating heart out of them and that sort of qualified as an adventure. Tommy nicknamed me "Fisherman" which I took as quite a compliment. We would see pilot whales sometimes and the Japanese divemaster reported a whale shark oceanside once.

One day I caught a marlin, a small one, and regretted it. It was nice reeling it in and getting it in the boat, but it was so strong, so alive, and so determined not to die that I realized later I should have asked that it be tagged and released. It was a beautiful fish and had plenty of fight left. Many of the expats were spear fishermen. I respect that, especially since there is nothing random about it. You select *the* fish you want for dinner and spear it. No by-catch, no undersized fish, just the one you want. I've eaten muk-tuk,[25] or whale, before when in the

Arctic and in general I have no problem with sustainable hunting of anything. But indiscriminate fishing for sharks, just for the fins, is a sin, as is any type of

---

24   A calming herb (commonly used in the Marshall Islands where it is legal).
25   https://en.wikipedia.org/wiki/Muktuk

whaling other than by indigenous people, as is elephant, or any other trophy hunting. Drives me crazy.

The Obama Administration was quite sympathetic to climate change and ocean issues. That was clear at the Chief of Mission conference, the annual gathering of U.S. Ambassadors from all over the world. The highlight of the conference for me, aside from being in the company of all of America's ambassadors at one time, was sitting at the lunch table with Ambassador Caroline Kennedy, then ambassador to Tokyo. I wanted to talk to her about Remembrance Day in the Marshall Islands, and tell her that I'd met one of the Japanese fishermen unlucky enough to be onboard the *Lucky Dragon*, the ship that wandered into the exclusion zone of the nuclear Bravo Nuclear test, the same test that contaminated Marshallese residents. The fisherman had spoken at the Remembrance Day ceremony. But it was a big table, and Ambassador Kennedy sat on the far side. Alas.

One of the perks of being an Ambassador is going to the annual Chief of Mission conference. President Obama rallied the troops during my tenure.

I did get a chance to encourage Secretary Kerry to visit the Marshalls by using great scuba diving and the rich, marine environment as bait, knowing his great interest in the oceans. "Yes, I'll have to do that!" he said. And, we almost got him, but other events intervened. North Korea tested a nuclear bomb and Secretary

Kerry cancelled the Marshall Islands stopover to work with Japan and South Korea on dealing with the North.

Scuba diving and snorkeling in the Marshall Islands was better than anywhere in the world, including Hawaii. I went with Hiro Uyeda from Ray Crew. The first time I saw sharks I first looked at the shark's behavior. It seemed uninterested in me. Then, I looked at Hiro's behavior. He was also casual. I followed his lead on how to behave. Calmly. No big deal. Hiro enjoyed seeing the sharks and rays and turtles as much as anyone, but he was really good at getting photos of tiny marine creatures; candy cane shrimp and little nemos endemic to the Marshall Islands. He would bring a little board on dives and write down what he was seeing. Usually, I had totally missed whatever Hiro had found hidden in the coral. Our favorite spot was the "aquarium" at the edge of the atoll near one of the passes to the sea.

On the way back from the Honolulu conference I logged onto my State Department internet remotely, using a "fob" with a temporary number that I entered for security. I got the word that I was not on the promotion list. So, I had made it to the Senior Foreign Service and equivalent rank of Admiral or one star general but that would be the high-water mark. In that same communication I saw the news that one of the students I recruited for the State Department as an intern had just made it through the security process after a long wait and would join the next A-100 class. She was on her way! We were allowed to find six talented students from underrepresented minorities and offer them paid internships. It was a great program, sadly, now discontinued. The second-generation American would be a great addition to the Foreign Service. And I'd make other plans. The best "other plan" has been work with the State Department's Inspector General's Office, and I've inspected Embassy Bogota, Embassy Copenhagen, and the South and Central Asia Bureau for the Office of the Inspector General. It's been a great way to stay involved and stay in touch on international issues.

There's an old adage that sooner or later the Foreign Service will break your heart. I imagine that's true. It reminds me that Kalia, who made deep attachments and found it hard to leave a post, once said. "Dad, I cried every time we moved, because I loved every place that we lived." I did too. A friend who retired when

I did said, "I wish I could put another quarter in and go on that ride again." It is the ride of a lifetime. I wouldn't mind starting over in A-100 and "doing it right" this time too. Sure, I'd put another quarter in.

Farewell Majuro!

Iokwe Aelop im kommol! It's been an honor to represent the United States in the Marshall Islands. I'm pleased to have been a friend of the Marshalls since August 2012. The U.S. will rightly be seen as successful if the Marshall Islands are successful. As a major development partner, we want to see the Marshalls continue on a path toward prosperity and greater independence with a vibrant, healthy, well-educated population. I know you will warmly welcome Ambassador Karen Stewart who brings a wealth of experience and enthusiasm to this great assignment. There are many Americans like me who have been touched by the people, the history, the culture and the beauty of the Marshall Islands, and who will remember your smiles, your sunsets, and your rich ocean home. Kathy, Bryan, Kalia, and I especially thank you. To my friends at USAG-KA, my utmost respect. To the Small but Mighty embassy, you all are the best. *Kommol, im bar lo kom.*

Whirlwind out!

———————◆———————

Q: As you then prepare to come back to the U.S. were there ideas that you had for sort of post State Department life?

ARMBRUSTER: We went back to Texas for a couple of years. In San Antonio I was flying little airplanes. That is a hobby of mine. Then I started working for the Office of Inspector General (OIG) and I've now led inspections of the South and Central Asia Bureau, Embassy Copenhagen, Embassy Bogota, and now embassies N'djamena, Chad, and Nouakchott, Mauritania. That is another great way to contribute. I really like Inspector General Steve Linnick's motto and driving vision: "Promoting Positive Change." We do that. We do a lot of offline counseling in the Office of Inspector General. We also write a "Spotlight on Success" where we find things being done really well that could be replicated elsewhere. In Bogota it was a color-coded security map down to the local level. So, if you were traveling to the north, for example, you would see areas that were safe and in the green, and dangerous ones in the red with information about previous security incidents. In Chad, we are looking at a U.S. funded elephant monitoring system to combat poaching as our spotlight.

We also come up with recommendations on where embassies can improve. I speak sometimes about climate change and just had a good session with Cornell University students, and I also do some writing. You saw the article *Practicing Environmental Diplomacy* in the Foreign Service journal. So I definitely try to stay engaged. I think I will always be recruiting in a way for the State Department. I think I joined it for the adventure, but I learned that service is its own reward. That is why I stayed in.

Q: OK, you were an ambassador and then you continued to look at the service from the critical eye of the Office of Inspector General.

How do you see it changing and are there recommendations you would make in general for how the State Department should function?

ARMBRUSTER: I have always wished that we could have a large cadre of people come into the State Department even for just a year or two to become familiar with what we do. When they talk about "Right Sizing" for most embassies that is like double the mission, because we do good work. When you have an economics officer or a commercial officer, they are going to bring in businesses and create revenue for the United States. So, embassies are good investments. I do believe in universality; we should be everywhere. We have interests everywhere in the world. So, we are doing that right. I think that public diplomacy is a powerful tool and the U.S. military leadership has often said they need diplomats on the ground too. One to mitigate conflict, but two, when there is conflict to help with the aftermath and development. So, I think we are underfunded. We have to continue to fight the good fight to promote the work to the public. I think students are very well informed but the average American probably doesn't have a great idea of what we do. What we accomplish throughout the world is something we should be proud of and something we should promote.

As for changes, as a career ambassador it would be good if we had a cap on political ambassadors. The American Foreign Service Association does a good job of lobbying and pushing back when those political appointee numbers get too high. There are good political ambassadors as well and sometimes they become spokespeople for the State Department. We just have to maintain the primacy of the State Department in foreign affairs. Make sure our voice is usually the deciding one in national security considerations, because we do have the experience, we speak the languages, often we have the depth to come up with good solutions to international problems. Those problems aren't going away.

Q: And with regard to training for State Department officers, is there a new direction you would recommend or different ways to train them?

ARMBRUSTER: Colin Powell said that coming into their careers, foreign service officers are better prepared in terms of education and experience than military officers. He said that by the time they get to the end of their careers the military officers have had more training and more leadership opportunities and are better equipped than we are because we spend so much time just getting the hands-on experience and less time training. I think what would be great is a dedicated training regimen where, after every tour, you have concentrated language or cultural training or whatever it is, commercial training, before your next assignment. The Foreign Service Institute does a great job. I think the language teachers are terrific. I took negotiations training here. That helped me negotiate better and was a real pivotal course.

We need to continue to invest in that. Foreign service officers shouldn't discount their time at FSI or in training or being seconded to another agency or to an American business or corporation. These opportunities are great as well as the war colleges. So, the opportunities are there, but we have to recognize they are worth the investment in terms of time and taking FSOs away from embassies. I am a big believer in training.

Q: Then the only other aspect is how the State Department acts interagency. I don't know how much you saw of that but obviously it is also a major issue for the department and our lessons learned, kind of from Iraq and Afghanistan, often go back to this question of how well the government thing worked.

ARMBRUSTER: The "whole of government" approach. I think that has become part of the ethos overseas. I do think the country team model works, and when people look at that and experience it hopefully they will bring that back to Washington and apply it. Every embassy is different. The military says if you have seen one embassy, you have seen one embassy. It is very personality dependent but I have always found overseas – maybe because of the proximity and working closely with your colleagues, playing sports with them – always seems to be collegial. Whether it is a big place like Moscow or a small mission like Havana, the agencies recognize that they are all there pulling in the same direction. You really never feel any kind of partisanship. It is all really very pragmatic, professional diplomacy that goes on overseas. I think that model works well.

Q: *Retirees, is there a moral role for them or, in your experience, is there a greater value that they could provide? Or is it simply better that when you retire you retire and leave opportunities for those coming behind?*

ARMBRUSTER: Yeah, there is kind of both sides to that. It is good to experience things outside of government. I volunteer on the board of Strategies for International Development, an NGO devoted to alleviating poverty. I traveled to India as a business consultant, but I still like being involved and I like being a resource for the OIG as long as they need me. I guess it is retiree dependent. Some want to go off and become farmers or do something completely different. But it is an honor to have a chance to serve and promote American values, help out American citizens when they are in trouble. It is a great career that I would recommend to anybody.

Q: *I think that is a great place to end. Thank you.*

End of interview

Now back in the "real world" I've traveled to India as a consultant, and I also write for several foreign policy outlets, along with inspector general work. Every now and then I get an email from a friend asking me to "talk them down," when they get discouraged about America's standing in the world. I've always cared deeply about how America looks in the world's eyes, but I know it's a big world out there and people recognize we are not perfect. And we are not the center of the world. There is a lot of localism for want of a better word. It doesn't matter where you live, people think they live in Universe Central. So, when America goes off the rails a bit, I know our values will put us back on track. Sooner or later. I wrote this the day after the 2016 presidential election for OpsLens, a new internet news source.

America in the World's Eyes, **OpsLens**. November 9, 2016
by Thomas Armbruster:

If Americans are in shock about Trump's win, imagine the discombobulation abroad. When Barack Obama was elected in 2008, it validated what the world believes, that the United States is a country that can live up to its founding ideals. President-elect Trump rocked the world because he rocks the foundations of America, challenging religious freedom and tolerance, challenging our historic inclusion of immigrants, even questioning our first allegiance to the world's strongest democracies, our allies, with whom we forged an international order, including NATO.

Like most Americans though, international audiences understand there is a difference between political rhetoric and reality. If a Trump administration can deliver a more competitive America that works in the international arena, he will be judged by that. Up until now, it has just been words. Some of them inflammatory, some of them disheartening, but ultimately just words. As of yet, there is no wall, there are no deportations, and no backing away from our commitments to our allies. We can get on course and lead the world as we should, given our resources, our history, and our capabilities.

This election also put each of us, and our beliefs, in stark relief with one or the other candidate. There was a real choice. And that is the beauty of democracy. Self-correction is part of the process and the American experience is a long-running show. So for the people who found hope in Hillary's and Bernie's messages, the answer is to get involved: locally, at the state level, nationally, and internationally.

Let me quote my friend from Finland. He says to Americans who are disillusioned, 'There is no "Canada" to go to. Instead, one should look the reality and the facts boldly in [the] eye – even if it scares the hell out of you – and continue working for the world one wants to see and the world one believes in. That is the only way forward. There really is no other alternative.' The other beauty of democracy is the ability to make our voices heard.

The U.S. has good friends abroad who want us to be the beacon for inclusion and democracy that we can be. Even in Mexico, a country that became a whipping boy for many domestic problems. Mexico is still one of our top trading partners. A real partnership with Mexico is vital for both countries. So hopefully the policy will be more accommodating than the rhetoric and President-elect Trump will find ways to reach out to our neighbors, work on an immigration policy that makes sense, and craft a new trade deal that doesn't shut the door. A few more bridges before we contemplate a wall.

One bright spot may be the opening this creates with Russia. As bizarre as this bromance between Putin and Trump may be, there is likely to be a "honeymoon" between the U.S. and Russia that should allow us to make real progress on Syria and to reduce the tensions and brinksmanship Russia has been practicing with the Baltics and elsewhere. Trade deals with Russia would be good for both countries, and lessening tensions would allow government funds to flow toward infrastructure rather than new Cold War toys and confrontation.

For the voters who put their faith in Trump's ability to make better trade deals and to bring manufacturing back to the U.S., the real test will be whether Trump can deliver on education, both higher education and vocational, to make disenfranchised workers competitive internationally. American companies don't take orders from the White House, but they do know they need an educated workforce to compete. Jumpstarting the Amer-

ican economy by investing in infrastructure, as promised, would also put Americans to work and make America more competitive.

Balancing the promises at home and abroad will mean tough choices on defense. Pulling back from our commitments abroad may save money in the short run but cede influence and markets to China and Russia. Trump's bottom line message though was not necessarily insular. The promise is to "Make America Great Again." America can't do that by pulling up the drawbridge and disengaging from the world. We can only do that by engaging.

I'll never forget being at a revolutionary rally in Riga, Latvia before the fall of the Soviet Union. Independence flags flew everywhere and the crowd in the rally was in the midst of fierce arguments with pro-Soviet and pro-independence people speaking their minds. I asked one of the participants to tell me what was going on. Almost immediately the crowd turned to me. Simply because I was an American. The crowd saw in America a great hope and promise. America was the standard they wanted to judge their own independence movement by. Before this moment, I never truly knew how powerful the idea of American democracy could be.

The last big disruptor of the political norm was Ronald Reagan. One of his favorite phrases was calling America a "City on a Hill." We are still on the hill. People around the world are watching. For all of us the responsibility is to help America live up to its best ideals. Let's be that beacon of light and hope on the hill.

Thomas Armbruster is an OpsLens contributor and former U.S. Ambassador to the Republic of the Marshall Islands. In his long career as an American diplomat, Thomas Armbruster served as the Consul General at the U.S. Consulate General in Vladivostok, Russia; Deputy Chief of Mission at the U.S. Embassy in Tajikistan; Principal Officer at the U.S. Consulate General in Nuevo Laredo, Mexico; Political Affairs Officer and Nuclear Affairs Officer at the U.S. Embassy in Moscow, Russia; and Vice Consul at the U.S. Interests Section in Havana, Cuba. Prior to joining the Foreign Service, he was a reporter for the CBS affiliate KGMB-TV in Hawaii. Mr. Armbruster holds a B.A. from

McDaniel College, an M.A. from St. Mary's University, and an M.S. from the Naval War College.

And I've stayed involved in environmental issues, particularly climate change. And again, this generation gets it and will do the right things. Our family enjoyed volunteering at the Coral Restoration Foundation in Key Largo, and I spoke to the American Mock World Health Organization in Atlanta in October 2016 about climate, the theme of their conference. Here's an excerpt:

Relocating coral

KEYNOTE ADDRESS

AMERICAN MOCK WORLD HEALTH ORGANIZATION
ATLANTA, GEORGIA, OCTOBER 2017

You invited me! What! Do you know how big my carbon footprint is? It's like bigfoot!! I eat gas for breakfast. I've got to plant like 50,000 trees just to offset the jets I've flown in around the world. I fly small planes for fun!

Well, seriously, we all live in the real world. We drive cars, fly in airplanes, use plastics, and all of the other modern conveniences.

But I do what I can. I bring my own grocery bags. usually. I avoid Styrofoam like the plague… usually.

And it did not seem right to fly to a conference to talk about climate change. I thought about walking it, but we settled on an electric car…. it was a great drive. You can ask my chauffeur and bodyguard and son Bryan in Q&A. But it took a little more effort. And that's the thing.

There are three things I'd like to do today: 1) introduce you to my climate heroes; 2) tell you about the Marshall Islands, one of the most vulnerable countries in the world to sea level rise; and 3) talk to you about international careers…

Coral around the world is subject to coral bleaching, when the water gets warmer, the coral dies.

Here we are relocating coral from a construction zone where they are mining coral to get to the sand to make concrete.

<Insert figure here>

I remember the little tropical fish would stay with the coral all the way to the surface. That's their home. Their life. And coral contributes to our lives too by being part of the ocean's food chain.

I said I had three climate heroes. The first is environmental filmmaker John Webster who lived without plastic products for a year and documented it in the film "Recipes for Disaster."[26] My second climate hero is Marshallese Foreign Minister, the late Tony deBrum who helped to get countries to agree to the ambitious goals of the Climate Summit in Paris and who fought for justice for the Marshall Islands over the nuclear testing legacy.

My third climate hero is you guys. This is the American Mock World Health Organization. You've got a million issues you could have chosen. But you chose climate. One of the toughest issues around. One that will require all of us to be creative. And to change. I'm impressed with you guys. And I want to follow your progress, so find me on Facebook and let me know what you're doing. How you're changing the world... I know you will.

You probably know that the U.S. is pulling out of the Paris Agreement, a voluntary arrangement that almost all of the world signed up to. But you might not know that in the meantime, states are signing up to it. Big states like California, so the fight is not over. And you can be part of it.

The climate deniers are a little like the doctors in the 50s who said smoking was good for you. You know it's common sense. If you smoke a pack a day, your chances of getting cancer and dying are increased. It's the same as if you pump pollutants into the atmosphere every day. The chances of bad things happening to the planet are also increased.

Sure, Uncle Joe smoked two packs a day and he's still going strong at 91, and sure, it snowed in north Texas, so there is still some cold air in the atmosphere. But let's not kid ourselves, we are playing a dangerous game by experimenting with the planet's resilience and ability to absorb CO_2.

---

[26]   https://filmsfortheearth.org/en/films/recipes-for-disaster

But I'm optimistic. I'm optimistic because humans are problem solvers. that's what we like to do. and we're good it. Send a man to the Moon. Roger that. Put an alarm clock, phone, camera, TV, and repository of all the cool things cats do on one device? No problem. Humans are smart.

One more thing. We need to all be in this together. Let's not get distracted by differences in skin color, religion, political party, or sexual orientation. Diversity is our strength in America. And in the end, we are all made up of the same atoms, the same stardust, the same dreams, and the same goals for our families.

I know your goal, the AmWHO goal, is to build a better, healthier future for people all over the world.

Crush it!

Work overseas...

Work for doctors without borders, or the flying doctors, or CARE, or [the] Peace Corps. You don't have to do it forever, but you'll find the time you spend helping others is time well spent for yourself.

I served for 27 years in the U.S. Foreign Service, working in Finland, Cuba, Russia, Mexico, Tajikistan, and the Marshalls. I know that we need experts on tropical diseases, HIV/aids, nutrition, disaster relief. We need environment, science, technology, and health professionals.

Go to careers.state.gov and have a look at the internships and career paths. I guarantee you'll find something you like.

November 9, 1975

Moscow, Russia

...So let me tell you about today... a new Foreign Service Officer named Marty came downstairs this morning and said it'd be nice if we could go somewhere. Being a kindly soul, and not having any special plans, I obliged to be tour guide for today. We went to the Kremlin (inside the walls) and it was a new experience for me because I had only been to Red Square which is outside the Kremlin walls. The inside is fabulous. It's on a slight hill and gives a good view of the river and the city. The inside courtyard is made of cobblestones and with a little imagination and the help of [the] 15th century building surrounding the courtyard it's almost possible to hear the horse carts clicking away on the cobblestones...

I'm listening to Simon and Garfunkel right now playing 'Homeward Bound' and I don't feel homesick. Because I know it's one year. That seems just about perfect for me... for now. I don't know if I'll become sick of this traveling to foreign lands or become caught up in the excitement of it. I've got to admit there's something exciting about waking up and stretching and all of a sudden realizing that Moscow is right outside. It's like the old-time explorers, I can see how they felt, 'what's over the horizon?' No one knows. That's what life is all about.

AFTERWORD

Odysseus sent his arrow singing through the axe handles in 7th grade for me. That was the life I wanted. Travel, adventure. Students have asked me thousands of questions over the years, but what it really comes down to is what would Foreign Service life be like for me? I hope this book gives some sense of the life of a Foreign Service Officer, from the first day as the embassy's lowest ranking American, to the last day as ambassador. As a Foreign Service Officer you'll put on more miles in your career than Columbus, and you could spend, like I did, 20 years abroad.

I'm no Henry Kissinger. This book is about day-to-day diplomacy. I started in a warehouse in Helsinki and finished on a tropical island in the Pacific. I'm a field guy with tours in Finland, Cuba, Russia (twice!), Mexico, Tajikistan, and the Marshall Islands. At one of the diplomatic class reunions (that I missed) my class voted me least likely to be spotted in Washington. And my one Washington tour was a two-year stint as polar affairs officer – as far from the swirl of insider Washington as you can get.

If you want to change the world though, the Foreign Service is a pretty good way to go. The experiences changed me, but I'm still at heart idealistic. Go figure. That's why I'm encouraging you to get involved. Becoming an ambassador is about presidential nominations, senate confirmations, and security clearances, but it's also representing something bigger than yourself. It's a privilege to work on the challenges we face. As a Foreign Service Officer you'll work on war and peace, women's issues, sports diplomacy, counternarcotics, intelligence sharing, and helping out Americans in trouble.

For me, environmental issues were central. I gained a global perspective on climate change. The Marshall Islands is one of the most vulnerable countries in the world to sea level rise. It is not the beach real estate that is precious. It's their culture, history, language, and identity at stake. They are Pacific islanders. Born of the Pacific and masters of the ocean. Ultimately, America will also be judged by our response to their crisis. Having detonated 67 nuclear blasts in the Marshalls during the Cold War, we have a special responsibility. We will lose too if the Marshall Islands go under. I hope the islands will stay beautiful coral necklaces in the Pacific Ocean. And I know the Marshallese won't go willingly. As President Loeak (predecessor to President Heine) told a crowd of international visitors, "If the waters come, they come. I'm not leaving."

There's always good work to be done for America in every part of the globe, from North

Korea, where we have to be tough with a brutal regime, to the South Pole, where the Antarctic Treaty is a model for international environmental cooperation. The first responsibility of any government is the welfare of its people, and overseas the front line more often than not is the U.S. embassy. From there we battle cyclops, listen to the sirens, and do our best to make our way home.